Smoking, Class and the Legitimation of Power, by Sean Gabb

First edition, February 2005

The right of Sean Gabb to be identified as the author of this work has been asserted hereby in accordance with the Copyright, Designs and Patents Act 1988.

Published by
The Hampden Press
Suite 35
2 Landsdowne Row
Mayfair
London W1J 6HL
England

Telephone: 0870 242 1712
E-mail: directors@hampdenpress.co.uk
Web: www.hampdenpress.co.uk
Directors: Dr Sean Gabb, Dr Chris R. Tame, Mario Huet

ISBN: 0 9541032 4 6

British Library Cataloguing in Publication Data: A catalogue record for this book is available from the British Library

CONTENTS

ACKNOWLEDGEMENTS

The Right To Smoke: An Historical View was first published by FOREST, London, 1990. *The Right to Smoke: A Christian View* was first published by FOREST, London, 1989. *The Right to Smoke: A Conservative View* was first published by FOREST, London, 1989. *Commercial Advertising: A Threatened Human Right* was written for the Campaign against Censorship, but—so far as anyone can tell—was never actually published. *Saving The Kiddies, Enslaving Adults* first appeared as *Free Life Commentary* No.73, October 2002, at : www.seangabb.co.uk/.

Front cover illustration: Henri-Edmond "Cross", *Self Portrait with Cigarette* (1880)

INTRODUCTION:
SMOKING, THE RULING CLASS
AND LEGITIMATION DISCOURSE

The three longest of the pieces here reprinted were written in 1988 and 1990 for the Freedom Organisation for the Right to Enjoy Smoking Tobacco (FOREST), which was then under the directorship of Dr Chris R. Tame. These received extensive coverage in the media at the time of publication, but are now out of print. Since there appears to be a brisk market in second hand copies—as evidenced by a search on Amazon—I have decided to bring them together in a new edition, and to add a few of my later writings on tobacco.

Looking back over 15 years, I am able to see many faults in the FOREST writings. Most obviously, there are faults of style. These were about the first things I had written for publication, and my first writings in several years. They were effectively the writings of a beginner. Now, it can take a writer many years to find his own style. Turning out sentences that read well each on its own is easy. Arranging them so they read both logically and smoothly, with the appropriate emphases and an overall uniformity of tone, is much harder. Whether I have achieved this now I am not able to judge. But I do know that I had not achieved it in 1988 or for several years thereafter. The style is often ponderous. Worse, it is often self-indulgent.

Another obvious fault is my referencing. This is a purely technical skill, and I do not think it boasting to say that I now have it as well as anyone else, and perhaps better than most. Back in 1988, I was plainly feeling my way. I was competent in referring to books – author, title, publisher, date and place of publication, and page or section number. But I wish I had taken more care with newspaper and magazine references. These can be found from the indications that I give, but I really should have given fuller indications.

More important, however, though perhaps less obvious, are the defects of my analysis. I deal well enough with the secondary reasons for the war on tobacco—puritanism, mistaken science, and so forth. But I had as yet given little thought either to the nature of modern class rule or to public choice economics. This means that I almost wholly overlook what I now believe is the primary cause of the war against tobacco.

Legitimising the State

In any society, the main function of government is to provide status and incomes for the ruling class. However recruited, the members of such a class will be motivated by a disinclination to earn their living by voluntary exchange, or by a delight in coercing others, or by a combination of the two. Its size and activities will be determined by the physical resources it can extract from the people, by the amount of force it can use against them, and by the nature and acceptance of the ideology that legitimises its existence. None of these factors by itself will be decisive, but each is a necessary factor. Change any one, and the working of the other two will be limited or wholly checked.

We can see this in many ancient and oriental societies. In these there was both unconstrained force available to the ruling class and a general acceptance of its legitimacy as a tool of government. But the extraction of resources was limited by an almost universal poverty. Even taxes and regulations that kept the people on the edge of starvation could finance only a tiny ruling class—and this is one reason why entry to the ruling class was so jealously policed by those within it. We can see it in much of 18th century Europe. Here, there was both a growing surplus to extract and various ideologies of submission. But governments were constrained in practice by the ability of their subjects to run away—either to neighbouring states where assimilation was fairly easy, or to the more distant colonies of the maritime powers. And we can see it in much of Protestant Europe during the Reformation. There was a surplus to extract often greater than needed to keep the secular authorities in their accustomed style of life, and there was considerable force available to governments. But these were insufficient to establish the new churches with all the wealth and privilege of the displaced Roman Church: no twisting of doctrine could be found to reconcile even the smallest independence of judgment with the old Establishment.

The Social Construction of "Social Problems"

There is a fourth, if subsidiary, factor. This is the ability to discover "problems" that allow practical applications of the legitimising ideology. Sometimes, these may be genuine problems—enemy threats, for example. More often, they are problems so obviously fabricated that later generations may have trouble understanding how anyone could have raised them or how anyone could have believed in them—heresy, for example, or witchcraft, or sexual nonconformity. But the specific content of problems is unimportant, so long as it appeals to the public opinion of those times and places where they are raised. What does matter is that the problems entail "solutions" that require government action. Better still, problems should be announced that appear so grave and so insoluble that they go beyond applying the legitimising ideology, instead enabling the emergence of a new and more useful ideology. Let us return to the example of enemy threats. Most people agree on the duty of government to defend against foreign aggression. But this agreement in itself does not justify any specific policy. That requires a specific threat. Let that be found and explained, and there can be heavy military spending, and wars of foreign conquest, and even a militarising of national life that would not otherwise have found justification.

When looking at past ages or foreign places, we can easily see this process. Because long term trends are concealed behind a mass of incidental detail, it is hard to see it in our own societies. For a long time, indeed, the fact of class domination was so relatively small that we could afford to believe it did not apply to us. But it does apply, if hardly ever so brutally as elsewhere.

Class Power and Class Legitimation

Since the 17th century, England, together—if often at second hand—with those countries influenced by England, has enjoyed a happy coincidence of circumstances. There has been a great increase in wealth, without until recently any matching growth in the claims of our ruling class. This was constrained for much of this period by a large colonial frontier, and then by reasonable ease of movement within a decentralised English world, parts of which were more or less actively in competition with each other. There was also a most unusual set of ideological forces. The ruling class in England had always legitimised itself as the custodian of an ancient and limited constitution. This legitimisation became more explicit with the political and religious settlement of 1689. From then on, the legitimising ideology of the ruling class was an ideology of resistance that placed broad limits on the size and nature of government. The right of a committee of landlords to hang poachers was indissolubly connected with the rights of everyone to *habeas corpus* and trial by jury. The established order of things was accepted by those outside the ruling class, because they were able to see with unusual clarity that government is about wealth and privilege for a few. It was accepted by the ruling class, partly because it was genuinely believed to be the embodiment of truth in human institutions—and, after all, it was—and partly because the more intelligent members of that class realised that any claims greater than the privileges of land ownership and a vague social primacy might—as had nearly happened during the reigns of the later Stuarts—raise up an alternative ruling class.

This order of things collapsed in England during the first half of the 20th century. The reasons for collapse are complex, and there is no room here to enter into the details. But economic growth had made possible the emergence of large groups who were by education qualified and inclined to join the ruling class, but for whom, given the severe limitations on government in England, there was no room. In consequence, they were attracted to diverse ideologies of state activism—socialism, imperialism, national efficiency, eugenics, and so forth—and they contributed to an intellectual climate within which problems might be discovered that could only be solved by an enlarged state. At the same time, there was a closing of frontiers within the wider English world, and escape became progressively harder. The process was accelerated by two great wars in which the old order was both morally and financially bankrupted. What might otherwise have taken over a century, or even avoided, was achieved within about 40 years, and the English experiment in freedom was brought insensibly to an end.

There was no defining moment of change—no oath in the tennis court or storming of the Bastille. At first, the increases in state power were slow. Ideology, though never decisive, is an autonomous force, and can operate for at least a while even when its coordinate factors have altered. For a long time, the groups challenging the old ruling class tried to imitate its manners and its general culture, and this meant some acceptance of those liberal values that were not seen as immediately inconvenient. To some degree, this is till the case. And it helped that the main ideologies of state activism in that century enabled a ruling class so parasitic that it consumed resources faster than they could be created. But the managed capitalism of the late 20th century has allowed what remains a stable equilibrium between parasite and host. The people are allowed to create resources. An increasing share of these is then extracted by the ruling class for the solution of problems consistent with the assumptions of the dominant ideology.

Paternalism and Class Legitimation

Because the phrase is still associated with an order that no longer exists, it is worth specifying that, in our own present civilisation, the ruling class is not made up of landowners and the non-executive dignitaries of the old church and state. Individuals from these groups may belong to the ruling class, but such membership will not be by virtue of position within the old social order—rather, it will be for other reasons. The ruling class in modern England is made up of those politicians, bureaucrats, lawyers, educators, and associated media and business people who derive income and status from an enlarged and active state.

And it is also worth specifying that the mass media are an integral part of the system. Whatever may have been in our more liberal past, the function of the media now is not to report reality, but to fabricate a parallel reality in which the legitimising ideology is taken for granted. Such propaganda is not usually so overt as that of the great totalitarian tyrannies of the 20th century. Techniques of influence have much improved since then. News is reported, and with seeming accuracy. The propaganda lies in the selection and presentation of news. A skilled journalist can cover a story in such a way that no fact is untrue, and dissenting views are reported in full—and still manage to produce an article so biased that it amounts to a lie. It is a question of selecting the right adjectives, or suggesting doubts or motives, of balancing quotations, of carefully taking words and opinions accurately reported but framing them in settings that suggest the opposite. But whether subtle or obvious, the collusion of the media is essential. Ruling classes have always had need of their tame intellectuals, to make and articulate their ideologies of legitimisation—to dress up mass-murder and kleptocracy as *parcere subiectis et debellare superbos*. But no ruling class before now has ever faced a wealthy and semi-educated majority that had the formal power to vote it out of existence. The media therefore are needed as effectively part of the ruling class, to help nullify democracy. The people are to be consulted, and their answers are to be taken as binding—but in all cases the answers are to be to questions asked by and debated among the ruling class.

As for the legitimising ideology, this has changed over time. It was once largely to do with the welfare of the working classes—with carrying out the supposed wishes of the majority. It is now much more about promoting "democratic values"—which mean that the actual or probable wishes of the majority can be set aside in the name of these higher values. They comprise that axis of anti-liberal, anti-western, anti-science, anti-Enlightenment and pro-collectivist values and coercive social engineering that we call political correctness. With the decline of traditional socialism, this has gained a growing and hegemonic role in most developed societies. As an ideology, it manifestly promotes the power and privileges of the ruling class. The ideology is used to stigmatise and demonise any dissenting opinion, and to censor and silence it; and information is socially constructed in order to balkanise society into alleged "victim groups" who provide tribalistic bases for the exercise of political power and the extraction of resources by the ruling class.

This is the main strand in the legitimising ideology, but an important and continuing strand beside it is the belief that it is the duty and therefore the right of the state to save people from their own ignorance or folly.

That explains the nature of the problems discovered over the past few generations. Many have not been problems at all. In nearly all other cases, they have been less serious than was claimed. An economy based on voluntary exchange is not inherently unstable and in need of programmes of demand management and a welfare state. People of different nationalities can live together without having to be bullied by law into pretending to love one another. We are not running out of natural resources, and our industrial pollutions do not threaten life on earth. There are no satanic child abusers. Sexual abuse of children is statistically insignificant. Smoking and drinking and consuming other drugs and fatty foods are at least less dangerous than is claimed, and there is no good reason to believe that passive smoking even exists. But whether a problem is real is far less important than whether the people can be brought to believe in its reality and in the need for solutions that justify income and status for the ruling class and its various client groups.

The War against Tobacco

Therefore the war against tobacco. Its function is to provide a set of plausible excuses for the extraction of resources from the people and for the exercise of power over them. There is nothing new or unique about this war. It has been waged on and off for centuries. It is similar to the established wars against alcohol and drugs, and to the gathering war against supposedly unhealthy foods. Though, with the decline of public rationality, we now have our own witches and heretics to be combated—or, to be explicit, our racists and our paedophiles—the regulation of lifestyle is still the most plausible set of excuses for enlarging the income and status of our ruling class.

To defend in this war, it is necessary to show that the specific claims of harm are unfounded. But it is also necessary to explain why, in the face of continuing and overwhelming refutation, the claims continue to be made.

In the writings here reprinted, I do make the first defence. I do argue that the specific claims of harm are unfounded or exaggerated, and that they can, so far as they really exist, be avoided by voluntary cooperation. But I do not make the second defence. I do not explain the overall forces at work in the war against tobacco. There are indications here and there that I am aware of these forces, but there is no foreground analysis. Such, I suppose, is the difference between a writer of 28 and one of 45—or perhaps it is just that the unfolding of events has made obvious what once was hidden behind the incidental details.

When I first wrote about tobacco, the main argument was over levels of taxation and over the right of the tobacco companies to advertise. These arguments are now lost. There is now a comprehensive ban on the promotion of tobacco. The tax on cigarettes is today so high that only extensive smuggling allows large sections of the working class to continue smoking. The new argument is over the right to smoke in places of public resort. The reply that most such places are privately owned, and that it is not for the authorities to decide what consenting adults do in private places, has already been brushed aside. The remaining force of liberal ideology has diminished much even in just 15 years. The next argument, I have no doubt, will be over smoking in the home. Within five years, there will be a serious campaign to ban smoking in any place where children are or are likely to be present. This will be an instance of what Stuart Goldsmith calls the "saving-the-kiddies" argument. This will be reinforced by changes to the building and general health and safety regulations. On the pretext of avoiding fires and other damage to property, local authorities will force their tenants into non-smoking agreements, and these will be made on pain of eviction, and policed with all the cheapness and ingenuity of our technological age. The insurance companies will impose similar obligations on private landlords and perhaps too on owner-occupiers.

It can be argued that the ruling class does not really want to ban smoking. After all, the tobacco taxes bring in around £10 billion, or about two per cent of all government revenue. How could this be replaced without a deeply unpopular rearrangement of taxes? There are several answers to this. The most obvious is that ruling classes are not monolithic abstractions, but consist of individuals and groups whose minute interests need not be in harmony. There are groups within and around the ruling class whose interests involve at least the close regulation of tobacco and of other products, and who are not concerned about the fiscal consequences. As said, we live in an immensely wealthy society, able to support a much larger ruling class than ever before. This brings a diversity and even conflict of local interests. We no longer live in a society so poor that the ruling class is small enough to have a commonality of interests—say, in the enforcement of the game laws, or in the maintenance of primogeniture. Though united in its essentials—of disdain for voluntary exchange and desire to coerce others—our own ruling class is too large for complete unity of thought and action.

Another answer is to agree that tobacco cannot be banned, and that perhaps this is known to the more reflective members of our ruling class. There are the fiscal consequences. And, as with other recreational substances, it is beyond the physical ability of any ruling class to enforce a ban. This does not mean, however, that the war against tobacco is in any sense a sham. It can be used very effectively to reduce those who continue smoking to a sense of guilt and self-loathing that makes them into obedient sheep in all other matters. I have sat opposite smokers in television debates, and watched them abase themselves before the anti-smokers. They cry out, in defiance of common sense and common experience, that they are addicts, hopelessly enslaved. They have no intention of giving up, and excuse themselves for this by never questioning the budgets and power of those who would have them give up.

The Futility of the Tobacco Companies

When I was writing for FOREST, it still seemed reasonable to hope that the tobacco companies would respond to the attacks on them by investing more of their profits in defence campaigns. I now see that this was to misunderstand the nature of big business. An entrepreneur who starts or inherits a business can be expected to defend it from attack. It is part of his life, and its loss would leave a void. An executive in a limited company has different interests. He has a salary to earn in his current position and a career that he may conceive in terms of functions rather than of products. He needs to ensure enough profit for his company to keep the shareholders happy. But he need not have any attachment to the company or to its products. He will be inclined, therefore, to respond to attacks with short term compromises. The long term result may be failure of the company and its entire sector, but this is not his concern. When defence seems cheaper than compromise, he may defend. The moment one of the costs of defence may be his own inability to move from company to company without having his earlier acts held against him, he will compromise.

Moreover, even granting a corporate interest, it should have been plain by the end of the 1980s that the tobacco companies had no objection to an advertising ban, and perhaps quietly welcomed one. Had any one of the companies stopped advertising of its own choice, it would have reduced its costs, but might also have lost market share to those that continued to advertise. If all could stop at the same time, they would reduce their costs while leaving relative market shares unchanged. The value of a ban on advertising was to prevent new entrants to the market. Though presented on all sides as an attack on the tobacco companies, the advertising ban has, in effect, increased the cartelisation of the sector. The companies make bigger profits because of maintained sales and lower costs. As with the financial costs of tobacco taxation, the information costs of the advertising ban fall on the consumers.

I am glad I took what money I could from the tobacco companies, which were always the main backers of FOREST. I did more with it to defend the rights of smokers than the companies would have done by themselves. I only wish I could get more from them today. Sadly, there will be nothing more.

Writings Reviewed

Now to the writings themselves. My history of tobacco prohibition is a competent summary. I could nowadays much improve it. Even at the time, I was unhappy with the structure. But it is good enough. It shows how the war against tobacco began almost with its first export from America, and that the war was fought with a savagery and disregard for truth that far exceeds any of the current battles.

The Conservative defence of the right to smoke was first published under the name of a Conservative Member of Parliament, but expresses opinions that, for the most part, I did hold at the time. I then believed that the agenda of the Thatcher Government was to liberate the British people, but that this agenda had been corrupted in various ways. I now believe the agenda was one of replacing a social democratic order that had turned out not to serve ruling class interests with another one that did. If this new order laid greater emphasis on market rationality, it was not inherently liberal, but only a more stable means of extracting resources from the people. It was what Dr Tame calls "a sophisticated mercantilism". Looking past the liberal rhetoric about "rolling back the frontiers of the state", one sees no reduction in the overall burden of taxes on ordinary people, an erosion of due process rights that set the precedent for the gross invasions of the Blair Government, the first real transfer of power from at least formally accountable national bodies to various supranational institutions, and the uncontested rise of political correctness as legitimising ideology. When I wrote my Conservative defence, I thought of Margaret Thatcher as a kind of Julian the Apostate. Despite her miserable ejection from office, I can see her now as a kind of Diocletian. She brought stability to what had been crumbling. She did not make government better—only more efficient. What I took at the time as blemishes on the agenda I now realise were the agenda.

The defence of advertising was commissioned by the Campaign Against Censorship, but was never published. Nor was I paid for it. My understanding is that the Executive Committee spent so long discussing whether to publish it that the piece went eventually out of date. I include it because it was written around the same time as the FOREST pieces, and adds to my discussion of tobacco.

I have a much higher opinion of my religious defence of the right to smoke, published by FOREST in 1989. Though one of the earliest, this is of all my writings the one with which I am least unhappy. Indeed, it is the only one that I am able to hope will survive me. Though formally about the right to smoke, it goes far beyond this. It is a meditation on the relationship between theology and politics. Its conclusion is that liberalism is the ideology most pleasing to God. I think this is true on any sensible understanding of the Christian faith. It is also a case worth making for its political effect.

Religion and Resistance

Ideology, as said, is seldom a decisive force in politics. But its force can be greatly increased by adding a religious sanction to it. I am, for example, strongly opposed to the introduction of identity cards. They are useless against crime or terrorism or any of the other evils for which they are said to be the answer. Their function is specifically to enable more effective supervision, and therefore control, over our actions, and generally to let us know for sure who is the boss. I have written extensively against the various proposals made over the past decade, and I have spoken out in radio and television studios.

Does this mean that I will refuse to carry an identity card, should they be introduced? The answer is that I will not refuse. We can all fantasise about playing John Hampden—fighting oppression in the full glare of publicity now, and with some hope of fame in the centuries to come. That can nerve us to face a single and short act of martyrdom. But the imposition of identity cards will not bring that sort of martyrdom—certainly not in England. Refusing to carry one will gradually make it difficult to join libraries, to open bank accounts, to make agreements with utility companies, to sign contracts for the sale of property. Identity cards will insensibly become the main or only form of identification in a whole range of transactions. After a while, those refusing to carry them will find it impossible to go smoothly about their daily business. And they will not face understanding or sympathy. The majority will grow used to showing their identity cards half a dozen times a day, will experience no regular inconvenience, and will never notice the humiliation. They will regard refusal to carry one as a sign of eccentricity, and will add their own sanction to those of the state. Will I, therefore, martyr myself in private every day for the rest of my life? I think not. I shall protest. I shall grumble. But I will eventually accept identity cards just as I now accept passports, driving licences and income tax returns.

Religious scruples entirely change the case. Let me believe that identity cards are the Mark of the Beast prophesied in *Revelation*, and nothing will persuade me to carry one. What is a nagging inconvenience in the life that is now, compared with the infinite punishments and rewards of the one that is to be? So what if the newspapers never publish my letters of protest, and if people see me as a bore and a lunatic? They are not my audience. Their opinion is unimportant. God is watching me, and God is my Judge. If I am refused a job because I have no identity card, or if I must produce a stack of alternative identification every time I want to pay my telephone bill, I will recall the martyrs in ages of more active persecution, and pray that, in these far milder if more protracted trials, I may show the same firmness of spirit.

All religion can place limits of some kind on size and nature of human government. The Christian religion, though, is almost designed for that function. It emerged in a world already civilised and already governed. During almost all its first three centuries, it was persecuted. When it eventually became the established faith of the Roman world, it continued to exist beside a government not of its own making, and it had administrative structures and a theology separate from that government. No integration at the top—no granting of legal privileges to the bishops, no proclamation of the Emperor as the Lord's Anointed—could remove the basic distinction between church and state. The texts "Render therefore unto Caesar the things which be Caesar's, and unto God the things which be God's" (*Luke*, 20:25), and "My kingdom is not of this world" (*John*, 18:36) set the principle of distinction in theological stone.

In many respects, the Imperial ruling class was more oppressive after the 3rd century than before. This was largely a consequence of the greater pressure on the northern and eastern frontiers, on the mistaken fiscal and economic policies employed to deal with this pressure, and on the decline of population thereby resulting. In some respects, though, the Imperial ruling class was under greater restraint. I do not mean by this that the Christian Emperors were less personally tyrannical than Tiberius or Caligula or Nero or Domitian or Commodus or Heliogabalus. They were, but while these earlier tyrants stand out luridly in the history of their ages, their misrule was largely confined to the murder and spoliation of others within the ruling class: some of them—Tiberius and Domitian, for example—were efficient and, within the prevailing assumptions, notably just rulers so far as the people were concerned. What I do mean is that the tyranny of the ruling class as a whole was moderated by Christianity. The treatment of slaves and conquered populations became less cruel than in the earlier period. There was more calling to account of corrupt and oppressive officials. The ruling class of the pagan Empire was frequently more indulgent and its financial exactions were less severe. But it was adamant in forbidding the emergence of any new institutions of what we call civil society—even to the point of forbidding the citizens of Nicomedia to set up a fire service funded by private subscription. Those institutions that already existed were permitted to remain—but only in form: the substance was insensibly drained from them. There was in this period no public opinion that placed impassable limits on government. There was no *imperium in imperio*.

The triumph of the Church introduced real balance into the Constitution. Constantine might surround himself with bishops, and shower gifts on them, and they might allow him to convene the first ecumenical council. But he could not have those bishops put to death. He could not lay hands on their corporate property. He could not prevent the formation of monastic orders all over the Empire, or make regulations for them. His successor turned Egypt upside down trying to get his hands on Athanasius. He faced a wall of popular resistance. Ambrose of Milan could force Theodosius I to do public penance for his sins. Philosophers for nearly a thousand years had been writing about a law separate from and superior to human government. Now, for the first time, there were mobs and preachers ready to insist on this to the government. There were places of sanctuary, and endowed institutions of resistance. As an institution, the Church of the late Roman world was a parodic variation on the *New Testament*. It was corrupt. It persecuted heretics. It reproduced all the faults of vulgar paganism, and fabricated meaningless theological distinctions that are with us still. Even so, it provided that world with its first effective limits to the power of government since the collapse of Athenian democracy.

This is what makes the political implications of the Christian faith so important today. That faith may be true. It may be false. But it will add tremendous force to any secular ideology with which it can be associated. It is Christianity that restrained the Roman state in its last centuries, that civilised the barbarians, and that humanised war and government and social relationships in our own civilisation. We face a ruling class with technological resources that none other has ever had. There is nowhere left for us to run—not, at least, until settlements can be established on the inner planets and in the asteroid belt. All we can hope at the moment is that the predations of this ruling class can be resolutely opposed. Secular liberalism has much truth on its side. But truth is often no defence against power—and hardly ever against organised power. Liberalism by itself is not enough.

Texts in Context

I turn now to the texts. If I were writing these today, I know that they would be very different. Reading them for the first time in 15 years, I find myself profoundly unhappy with them. Indeed, all that has prevented me from rewriting them is idleness and the certainty that I shall be just as unsatisfied, if I set now to work, if I am still alive to read them again after another 15 years. Therefore, though I have standardised the references, I reproduce here everything in the main text much as I wrote it at the time. The defence of advertising is reproduced exactly as I wrote it. The history of tobacco persecution was heavily edited by someone at FOREST, so that about a third was cut out. Here, I follow my own text. The religious and conservative defences are a different matter. These also were edited. Sometimes, the cuts made were improvements. Once or twice, they disrupted the flow of the argument. Because my original files were saved on disks and in a format that makes it impossible to recover them, and because the only manuscripts are in faded dot matrix print that will not easily scan, I have decided to follow the texts as published by FOREST—though I have silently replaced some of the cuts which I think were unwise. Also, of course, I have corrected various typing mistakes.

Chris Tame: His Part in My Downfall!

Finally, I wish to record my thanks to Dr Tame. As said, the religious and conservative defences were my first writings for several years. I had passed most of my twenties wanting to write and believing I could be a good writer. I did write a novel, which was never published and which has now probably faded from the 5¼" disks on which it was stored, and I published two volumes of poetry in very limited editions. Apart from these, however, I had done nothing. I was cut off from the libertarian movement, only occasionally renewing my subscription to the Libertarian Alliance; and the local Conservative association saw me as useful simply for knocking on doors come election time. I knew that I should do something, but lacked the motivation to do anything.

In October 1988, I went along to a conference at the Imperial Hotel in London, where I saw Dr Tame and Brian Micklethwait for the first time in many years, and was reduced to envious despair when I saw so many people of my own age or younger who were making names for themselves as writers and activists. Nobody knew me there. Nobody seemed to care who I was. I was just another of those young men who turned up in the 1980s to libertarian events and were useful to fill seats and ask the occasional question, and perhaps to bore others with their ill-formed opinions of what was happening in the world and what ought to be done about it.

I was surprised therefore on that morning in December when I received Dr Tame's commission. Why had he asked me to do something so important? What on earth could he see in me? I had no idea. But while he was offering me a derisory fee for each defence, I knew that this was an opportunity not to be refused, and I set to work with a will. I had both finished by the end of the month, and I almost wept with joy when I saw them published and then discussed in the newspapers.

This was the beginning of my life as I had always wanted it to be. For that, I was and always will remain grateful to Dr Tame. But for him, I might still be a bored and frustrated legal civil servant. Thanks to him, I was hounded from my job within two years, and have never had an entirely regular career since. I have been scorned as a fanatic. I have been libelled by the newspapers. I have seldom been more than one mortgage payment from disaster. I have even, under the influence of the sources he fed me from FOREST, taken up smoking. To some, this may sound like a hint of blame. But there is none intended. I have enjoyed every minute so far. Accordingly, I dedicate this entire volume to him.

Sean Gabb
January 2005

1. THE RIGHT TO SMOKE: AN HISTORICAL VIEW

I: A Purely Private Affair, But...

On Monday, the 18th of September, 1989, the United Kingdom division of the Ford Motor Company made a rather significant change to the terms on which 12,500 of its office staff were employed. It announced that, as of the following January, they would be banned from smoking anywhere at work but in designated areas—and here only "provided it [did] not adversely affect those in the non-smoking areas"[1]

I took note of this announcement neither because I was likely to be affected by it, nor because I am someone who believes in the right to light a cigarette in any place, at any time, regardless of the wishes of others. I do not work for Ford, nor probably ever will. I am not a smoker. With the exception of snuff—which I take mentholated for my sinuses, and which is not currently under attack from any quarter[2]In passing, I might add that there are dangerous brands of snuff. The Bavarians have, or had, one called Schmaltzer, having a

---

[1]*The Daily Telegraph*, London, 20th September 1989.

[2]In 1970, it was stated to Parliament that "there is no evidence whatsoever to indicate that snuff-taking is harmful" (*Hansard*, 15th December 1970). This opinion has been repeatedly endorsed by Dr M.A.H. Russell, an expert whose writings against smoking are frequently published in the *Guardian* (for a detailing of his more extravagant and absurd claims, see my *The Right to Smoke: a Religious View*, FOREST, 1989, £1.00—and, I might say, worth every penny). For his evidence regarding snuff, see: *The Lancet*, 1st March 1980; *The British Medical Journal*, 26th September 1981; *The Lancet*, 14th December 1985). So far as I know, no one has even hinted that there might be any danger from passive snuff-taking. In 1978, accepting the evidence, and hoping to shift consumption from a tobacco product considered dangerous to one as yet found perfectly safe, the Government exempted snuff from excise duty. The resulting difference in price is worth bearing in mind. My smoking friends lay out an average of £10 per week on cigarettes. £5 has bought me enough snuff to last the rest of the century.

base of Brazilian tobacco flour, to which lime and lard and powdered glass are added. Clearly, though, the danger here is not in the tobacco.—what experience I have had of tobacco products I have usually found unpleasant. I readily admit that some of them are almost certainly bad for the health. My interest in tobacco, and in all the news regarding it, stems almost entirely from libertarian principle. I believe that people should have the right to do with themselves as they will, regardless of any possible harm to them. Any calculation of risk is for them alone to make. Even if it could be shown that non-smokers were endangered by the exhalations of smokers—and the present evidence is such that only fools and fanatics could ever accept it[3]—there would be no case for State action, but only for a more urgent formulation of private arrangements.

Arguing on these grounds, I cannot, and will not, claim that Ford had no right to impose its ban. There was no question of liberty involved. One group of people—namely the Directors of the Company—announced the terms on which it would continue to associate with another group of people—namely the Company's office staff. So far as I am aware, the Company enjoys no government subsidy or special protection of the sort that would justify my intervening as a concerned taxpayer. Nor, to my knowledge, have I any money invested in the Company. I can, as a consumer, boycott all Ford products until the ban has been removed—and I probably will. Beyond this, I readily admit, what

[3] As it happens, there is no good evidence for there being any risk from "passive smoking". It is forever being claimed that such evidence has been found, and sceptics are referred to the *Fourth Report of the Independent Scientific Committee on Smoking and Health*, a 68 page document published by the Government in the March of 1988. This Report does, indeed, support the claim, that a non-smoking spouse of a smoker runs somewhere between a 10% and 30% greater risk of contracting lung cancer than the non-smoking spouse of a non-smoker. But, if we look to this support, rather than what is most often piled on it, we see that the risk of lung cancer is estimated to rise from 10:100,000 to 12 or 13:100,000. In the first place, only a fool or a fanatic without regard for common sense could panic at a risk so trivial. In the second, a statistical variation so wide may be taken as pretty meaningless (See T.E. Utley, "Morality overcome by fumes" *The Times*, London, 29th March 1988).

Ford did was none of my business.

Even so, I was greatly disturbed by the news. For, though in itself a private decision, this was claimed as a victory for one of the most ludicrous yet sinister organisations in British public life. Ford, by its own choice, put restrictions on smoking among a large portion of its staff. The leaders of Action on Smoking and Health loudly and promptly applauded. If Ford had been compelled by law to restrict smoking, I have no doubt that they would have applauded no less loudly or promptly. All that would have been different was the object of their applause—the Government this time, rather than a board of directors. We are dealing here with people to whom the normal distinction between what is and what is not one's own business is a meaningless quibble. Consider how David Simpson, the Director of Action on Smoking and Health, greeted the news of the Ford ban: "For the first time" he enthused, "I really feel there is no stopping us".[4]

II: The Questions

i: The Desired End of the Anti-smoking Movement

What I propose in this paper to do is ask two questions. First, I ask: what is meant by these words—"there is no stopping us"? What, for these people, would represent final victory in their war against tobacco? The answer is simple: it would be a full prohibition, in public and in private, laid on the use of tobacco. Simpson, I grant, for all his other faults, is no fool. He knows perfectly well how far he can go in his public statements; and, if he ever reads my accusation, and thinks the effort worthwhile, he will deny it. "When did I ever call for this?" he might ask. "When did I ever call for more than tighter curbs on advertising, and on smoking in public, and for higher taxes on tobacco products"?

If I ever were drawn into a debate of this kind, I might answer that Mr Simpson has used words that, given their plain, grammatical

---

[4] Maurice Weaver, "Stubbing out the habit", *The Daily Telegraph*, London, 20th September 1989.

meaning, do call for prohibition. Appearing on the Channel Four programme, "Right to Reply", on the 17th February, 1990, he declared that "if cigarettes were invented today, there's no way they'd be allowed to be made, never mind advertised or promoted in any other way.... No decent society would actually allow, willy nilly, the promotion of a product even a tenth as dangerous as cigarettes. So that's why we want to ban them".[5] But this is at variance with his other recorded statements; and I can imagine that he would, if confronted with it, claim that words uttered unscripted on television ought not be given their plain, grammatical meaning—that the plural object of the verb "ban" was not intended to be cigarettes, but the activities of their advertisers and promoters. All things considered, I am inclined to accept this conjectural excuse. Showing Mr Simpson an indulgence that he would never show me, I overlook his one departure from a general policy of caution5. But I hardly need do otherwise. Taking only his considered public statements, we see the grossly illiberal nature of his movement's aims.

In plain English, "curbs on advertising" mean censorship. There is no difference in principle between forbidding a cigarette advertisement and forbidding an attack on the Government. Both involve the telling of a publisher what he can and cannot do. Curbs on the public use of tobacco require a violation of property rights, since many "public places"—cinemas, theatres, restaurants and so forth—are in fact privately owned. Where the lower income groups are concerned, I fail to see where a higher excise duty on cigarettes is likely to differ from an outright ban on their sale. The burden of the taxes already put on raises prices by an average of 200 per cent. I

---

[5]While quoting from statements made on television, I might as well add the words of Ms Joyce Epstein, the Assistant Director of Action on Smoking and Health. Asked on the BBC programme, "Over to You", on the 12th August, 1989, whether cigarette should be banned completely, she answered that there was "no right to smoke". This is, of course, ambiguous. She might have been saying, that we have no right to do what she considers bad for us. Alternatively, she might have been giving voice to the dreadful—and perfectly un-English—notion, that whatever is not specifically allowed by the law is forbidden. In either case, I scarcely need say, she would be hard put to raise any principled objection to Stalin or Hitler.

doubt whether raising them to the point where a packet of twenty cost £5 or even £10 or £20 would come near satisfying the clamour made every Budget Day.

And, illiberal as these aims are in themselves, they point quite clearly to the one final aim of prohibition. Anyone who believes that the more dedicated members of the anti-smoking movement want less than this has been taken in by the velvet glove. For the moment, the means used are largely indirect. The intention is to squeeze smokers into a small minority. But, once this minority is small enough, the iron fist will most surely be produced.

As evidence for this, recall the fate of Skoal Bandits—those strange tobacco bags that were to be put in the mouth and sucked. These never caught on. They were plainly a minority taste. Without their millions of users to defend them, they were fair game. At the first hint of evidence linking them with mouth cancer, up went the cry for prohibition. The cry was effective. The sale of oral snuff became a criminal offence on the 13th of March, 1990.

Recall, again, the impending fate of Senior Service, Capstan and Gold Flake cigarettes—brands which, on account of their tar content, have been declining in popularity for years. On the 13th of November, 1989, the Council of Ministers in Brussels proposed a maximum limit of 15mg of tar per cigarette, this limitation to come into effect at the end of 1992, effectively prohibiting the sale of the brands just mentioned.[6] Commenting, a spokesman for the Tobacco Advisory Council said: "What we are seeing by this EEC legislation is virtually the end of untipped cigarettes in the UK.[7] His comment fell short of the probable truth. It was further decided that, from 1997, the limit would be reduced to 12mg of tar per cigarette. What brands this will prohibit I am for the moment unaware—though only a little tightening more of the ratchet on this scale will leave even Rothmans and Benson & Hedges dangerously exposed. The only objection

---

[6]*The Daily Telegraph*, London, 14th November 1989. It may be of interest that strong cigarettes will remain on sale in Greece until 2006.

[7]*Ibid*

was—as might be expected—put up on behalf of the British Government. Its objection, however, was grounded not on any regard for the traditional, and bloodily earned and defended, rights of Englishmen, but on the claim that matters of health ought to be decided by the national governments of the Common Market: the only question debated was whether we should be oppressed from Brussels or from London. In these respects, the banning of tobacco products is no future possibility, but has already begun.

ii: The Intellectual Pedigree of the Anti-Smokers

When I first heard the term "health-fascism" used to describe the anti-smoking movement, I felt some doubt as to its propriety. The word "fascist" had been so overused that it seemed to have lost all meaning, save as a strong but vague pejorative. But, on reflection, I realised that, in this case, I was wrong. For such intellectual pedigree as the anti–smokers have they can plainly trace, not to anything English, or even anything within the more general Western tradition of the past two centuries, but to German National Socialism.

Almost whatever fad these "concerned middle-class progressives" take up, and publicise through the pages of *The Guardian* and *New Statesman and Society*, the followers of Adolf Hitler took up before them. Animal rights, vegetarianism, whole-grain bread and other "organic" foods, natural childbirth—each of these had as its first modern promoters the National Socialists. It is the same with smoking. Hitler and Himmler were both extreme haters of tobacco, and would have no one smoke in their presence. The Party ideologues, looking at its real and imagined dangers to health, condemned it as a "race poison" and called for restrictions.[8] Unlike

---

[8] Among the imagined—or, at least, the unproven—dangers of tobacco, consider the following: In the *Hamburger Frendenblatt* (22nd March 1944), an article was published by one G. Wenzmer. Called "Should Women be Allowed to Smoke?", its argument was that smoking damaged the ovaries. It was stated that marriages between heavy smokers produced an average of .66 children, while marriages between non-smokers produced an average of 3 children—Cited, Richard Grunberger, *A Social History of the Third Reich*, Weidenfeld & Nicolson, London, 1971, p. 264.

the leaders of Action on Smoking and Health, they had no need for mealy-mouthedness; but they openly attacked as a "liberal perversion" the view that one should have the right to dispose of his body as he saw fit—the *Recht auf den eigenen Körper.* They spoke instead of the "obligation to be healthy"—the *Pflicht zur Gezundheit.*[9]. Since health was now an integral part of the German national interest, they argued, it could no longer be possible to tolerate substances damaging to society as a whole, whatever the wishes of those individuals consuming them.[10] Compare with this the words from 1980 of Sir George Young, then a junior health minister in the government of Mrs Margaret Thatcher:

> The traditional role of politicians has been to prevent an individual causing harm to others, but to allow him to do harm to himself. However, as modern society has made us all more interdependent, this attitude is now changing.[11]

When, in 1944, F.A. von Hayek delivered his famous warning, that England was coming more and more to resemble Germany, he was laughed at. What better proof could be wanted, though, than the debate on smoking to show the gradual eclipse of our traditional regard for individual rights by an imported authoritarianism?

iii: Whether the End can be Achieved

But this is to digress. Having settled that the probable, if not yet the unambiguously stated, aim of the anti–smokers is to ban tobacco, I move to my second question, which is: whether these people are likely to succeed? If I look only over the course of my own life, and of the decade or so preceding my birth, I might feel that I had to answer "yes". Except where the revenue is concerned, they have won the

---

[9] From Robert Proctor, *Racial Hygiene: Medicine under the Nazis,* Harvard University Press, Mass., 1988, p. 248.

[10]*Ibid,* p. 240.

[11]Quoted in Heather Ashton & Rob Stepney, *Smoking: Psychology and Pharmacology,* Tavistock Publications, London, 1983, p. 144.

backing of the State. The tobacco companies have been compelled, under threat of legal sanctions, to adopt a "voluntary" code of advertising conduct. They have been compelled—in part by law, in part by unlawful pressure—to cry down their products by putting health warnings over them. Central and local government both spend large sums of our money on propaganda against smoking. Various pressures are being put on government employees not to smoke at work.[12] There have been actual prohibitions. If, taking only this into account, I look ahead, I see every reason for gloom. The anti-smoking movement seems to be in the position of an army that, after a long and closely fought battle, is on the point of scattering its enemy. "There is no stopping us" says David Simpson. He really does believe that a time will inevitably come—and sooner, perhaps, rather than later—when no one shall ever more need to scrub the nicotine stains from his fingers.

This is a horrible and a depressing prospect. But I doubt whether I, or anyone else currently alive, will ever see it. There have been customs that, observed by millions in generation after generation, have died out with the advance of our knowledge, or have been suppressed by overwhelming force. But I doubt whether the use of tobacco will become, or be made, one with touching for the King's Evil in England, or the binding of women's feet in China. It is something wholly different. If we confine our view to the past forty years of shrill campaigning, we shall be able to plot a line leading inexorably to prohibition. But, if we look instead over the entire period, of which the past forty years have been less than a twelfth, since tobacco and the Old World made each other's acquaintance, we

---

[12]Take, for example, Gloucestershire County Council, which has given its employees two years in which to give up smoking. Failure to give up will bring dismissal (*The Daily Telegraph*, London, 6th October 1989). Take also one of the sections in the Chancery Division of the High Court of Justice. In the January of 1990, the Chief Clerk there imposed a ban on smoking, on the understanding that separate facilities would be provided for smokers. By the following August, no such facilities have yet been provided—though, in possible compensation, the ban has from time to time been suspended. The Lord Chancellor's Department as a whole is currently going through some openly farcical process of "Consultation" preparatory to imposing a general ban.

shall see solid reasons for optimism. We shall see that the appeal of tobacco to those using it has always been so immediate and profound that any hope of outlawing it has been utterly vain.

III: Tobacco and Mankind

i: The European Discovery

It was shortly after Friday, the 12th of October, 1492[13] that the acquaintance was made. On this day, after a voyage of seventy one days, Christopher Columbus had his first sight of the Americas. Around noon, he with his senior officers set foot On Watling Island and raised the Cross and the flag of Castille, claiming possession of the country in the name of Ferdinand and Isabella, the joint monarchs of a Spain only lately reconquered from Islam but rapidly becoming the first power of Christendom. The natives who came down to the shore to watch this ceremony had, for the moment, no idea of its meaning; and, assuming that the strangers had come in peace, made welcome offerings of beads and choice fruits and other objects considered valuable.

Among these objects were the dried, yellowish, strangely aromatic leaves of an unknown plant. The sailors took these along with all else that was offered, but, seeing no use for them, threw them overboard into the sea. What they were there chiefly in search of was gold. It was their desire for riches that had supported them during an Atlantic crossing of 71 days. By and large, they went home disappointed. But, if it was the crimes of Cortez and Pizarro that were to unleash the great, and ultimately ruinous, flood of bullion into the Iberian Peninsula, Columbus and his men had still found gold after a fashion.

---

[13] It was actually the 21st October, the true 12th having fallen the Wednesday but one previously. All European dates before the calendar reform of 1582 are still given in the Old Style, which, by the end of the fifteenth century, had lost nine days since 325 AD. This is a trivial point; but, as it will doubtless be argued over ad nauseam in the correspondence page of *The Times* in 1992, I might as well make it here in advance of everyone else.

ii: Smoking before Columbus

It would be wrong to say that the practice of smoking dates from here. Much had long since been known in the Old World about the various uses of smoke. From the earliest times, incense had been burned as an accompaniment to worship. Its use, so far as can be told, began in Egypt or Babylonia, and was copied by the other nations of antiquity. When, for some transgression, God smote the wandering Israelites with a plague, it was with an offering of incense that His wrath was turned aside.[14] Later, in the Temple as Jerusalem, a vase of the costliest incense burned day and night outside the Holy of Holies. Among the Greeks and Romans, its price rose so high that the Alexandrian frankincense refiners were sealed into their working clothes, but were still stripped and searched at the end of their shift.[15] During the middle ages, both the Christians and the Moslems continued the practice of burning incense, and have continued it to this day. But, pleasant as its smell might often be, a stick of incense has few uses beyond the ceremonial or the fumigatory.

The Priestess of the Oracle at Delphi is said to have uttered her prophesies while drunk on the vapours that issued from a cleft in the rocks beneath her feet. No such cleft has ever been found, and it seems likely that whatever she inhaled was brought in by the priests whose living it was to put her ravings into competent, if often meaningless, hexameter verses. But, though respected, hers was not a popular office. Few held it willingly.[16] Nor were the observed effects of her smoking such as to encourage imitation.

Smoking was recommended by the doctors, but could never have been done with much pleasure. The smoke from burning hare's fur

---

[14]*Numbers*, 16:46-50.

[15]Pliny the Elder, *Naturalis Historiæ*, Bk. XII, cap. xxxii.

[16] Some oracles were staffed by means purely coercive. See, for example, Trimalchio's reminiscence: "Oh, with my own eyes, I've seen the Sybil at Cumae hanging in her cage. And when the boys used to ask her 'Sybil, what do you want', she would answer 'I want to die'" (*Cena Trimalchionis*, cap. 48).

was given as an expectorant.[17] Burning goat's horn was used to diagnose epilepsy.[18] For consumption, there was the smoke, inhaled through a reed, of dried dung from an ox fed on grass.[19]

Herodotus, describing the bathing habits of the ancient Scythians, tells how they would make a little tent by wrapping a woollen cloth round a tripod of sticks, and inside place a dish of red hot stones. "Then they take some hemp seed, creep into the tent, and throw the seed on to the hot stones. At once it begins to smoke, giving off a vapour unsurpassed by any vapour-bath one could find in Greece. The Scythians enjoy it so much that they howl with pleasure. This is their substitute for a bath in water, which they never use".[20] While an improvement on smoking dried ox dung, this vile custom remained exclusive to the Scythians. Elsewhere, except in those places where, with the decline of civilisation, bathing came to be given up altogether, personal hygiene was ensured by immersing the body in hot water and then anointing it with oil.

Much was known in the Old World about the practice of smoking. Quite understandably, since there was no tobacco, there was no idea of the habit of smoking. Eccentric claims have been made, but we are quite certain that tobacco was unknown. The genus Nicotiana, of which the most popular and widely cultivated species is now the *tabacum*, is native in its original state only to the Americas. In common with the potato, the tomato, the egg-plant and the chilli pepper, all members of the great solanaceæ family of plants, its

---

[17]Pliny, *op. cit.*, XXXVIII, liii.

[18]*Ibid*, lxiii.

[19]*Ibid*, lxvii: "[in casu phthisiscis] fimi... aridi sed pabulo uiridi pasto boue fumum harundine haustum prodesse tradunt". Later in his work (XXIX, v), Pliny alludes without evident irony to the popular funerary inscription "turba periui medicorum" (I was finished off by the doctors).

[20]Herodotus, *The Histories*, translated by Aubrey de Sélincourt (revised, A.R. Burn), Penguin Books, Harmondsworth, Middlesex, 1972, p. 295 (in the original—D, lxxiv- lxxv).

introduction to the European palate had to wait until after Columbus had made his voyage across the Atlantic.

iii: Tobacco in America

How and when it was first used in America no one knows. What accounts we have are fables rather than history.[21] Perhaps there was a single discovery the news of which was spread. Perhaps, as with fire and farming, there were many parallel discoveries. All that we can tell is that tobacco was already known around the start of the Christian era, and that its use was gradually adopted throughout the nations of central and most of north and south America. It was used by the Mayans. While the subjects of Hadrian were courting favour with gifts of incense to the unfortunate but deified Antinous, the cultivated inhabitants of southern Mexico were smoking crude cigarettes. They had no rice paper, but would wrap their tobacco in palm leaves or corn husks; or they would use reeds or bamboo; or they would use tobacco leaves and roll cigars. It was used by the Indians further north. They made pipes for themselves—sometimes with bowl and stem, to be held in the mouth, sometimes shaped like a Y, the forked extremities to go in the nostrils—and smoked their tobacco with other plants to vary its flavour or to make it go further. The Aztecs both smoked and snuffed. Elsewhere, tobacco was chewed, eaten, drunk as an infusion, or rubbed into the body. Excepting the hypodermic injection of nicotine—a means of administration never as yet become popular—our own uses of tobacco were all discovered long ago in America. The rest of mankind had only to imitate.

---

[21]21. One Huron legend, for example, tells how, long before the coming of the white man, there was a great famine over the land. All the tribes came together in a council and called on the Great Spirit Manitou for help. In answer, a beautiful and naked girl descended from the clouds. Leaning on her palms, she sat on the ground before the people, and announced that she was sent to bring food. This said, she returned into the sky. Where her right palm had been, corn sprouted, and where her left had been, potatoes. But from where she had sat tobacco appeared (see W. Koskowski, *The Habit of Tobacco Smoking*, Staples Press Ltd, London, 1955, pp. 39-40). Much as this may appeal to the imagination, it is probably not true.

iv: Its Spread Throughout the World

This was done as briskly as the slow communications of the day would allow. During the early years of the sixteenth century, as Europeans crossed the Atlantic in growing numbers, or stayed at home and read the travellers' accounts,[22] the habit of "smoke drinking" attracted a certain interest. The first white man to try it for himself may have been Rodrigo de Jerez, who had sailed with Columbus in 1492. Certainly, by the early years of the new century, many of the Spaniards living in Hispaniola had taken to smoking cigars.

a: Portugal

Yet, if it was the Spanish who first took up the use of tobacco, it was the Portuguese—still, before the rise of the Dutch and English, the masters of international commerce—who did most to convert the rest of the world. It was in Portugal that the tobacco plant was first cultivated outside of the Americas, its introduction having occurred around 1512. By 1558, snuff was on sale in the markets of Lisbon.

b: France

It was from here that the French received tobacco. In 1559, one Jean Nicot of Nîmes, arrived in Lisbon, sent to negotiate a marriage between the young King of Portugal and the French King's daughter, its purpose being to cement an alliance against the now overwhelming power of Spain. The marriage never took place; but Nicot, eager to keep his government informed of anything new or unusual, did send specimens of the tobacco plant back to Paris. Although it was at first called *l'herbe du Grand Prieur*, in honour of the Church dignitary by whom the specimens had been sent, the French by 1570 had settled on the modern botanical name for the plant of *Nicotiana*.[23] Within a few years also, they had become inveterate

---

[22]The earliest extant account of smoking is given by Romano Pane, the Papal missionary, in his *De Insularium Ritibus* of 1497.

[23]This is given in *L'Agriculture et la Maison Rustique* of that year by the brothers Liebault. For a few centuries, it went among some medical writers under the

snuffers. Tradition relates that it was Charles, Duke of Lorraine, who was the first Frenchman to take to the habit, his own consumption rising eventually to three ounces per day.[24] In any event, snuff was all the rage at Court by the second decade of the seventeenth century.

c: Italy and Elsewhere

Again from Portugal, tobacco was introduced to Rome. The Papal Nuncio at Lisbon—perhaps following Nicot's example—sent specimens to his master, Pius IV. Next, it travelled to the other Italian cities, and from there into Germany, Hungary, and the other nations of northern and central Europe, where its spread was greatly hastened by the unusual movements of armies and populations occasioned by the Thirty Years War.

d: England

Although the claim has been made, it was probably not from Portugal that it came to England. Not only had the English quite early begun their own exploration of the New World, but their settlements in Virginia were founded among pipe-smoking Indians; and, when tobacco made its appearance in England, during the third quarter of the sixteenth century, it was smoked in pipes, and the Portuguese were only later smokers rather than snuffers. It may be, then, that the habit was brought direct from America—and, as he boasted, was brought by Sir Walter Raleigh.

---

name of petum, which appeasrs to have been derived from an ancient Brazilian word for the plant. The etymology of the vulgar names of tobacco, tabac, taboc etc. is rather less easily settled. It might derive from the place names of Tobasco or Tobago; or from Toboca, the name of the Y-shaped pipe through which some of the Indians smoked. Other explanations have, from time to time, been suggested. But, rather than go though these, it seems fairer to say that no one knows the origin

[24]As a man who has taken six months to get through half an ounce, I find this rate of consumption almost incredible. Yet I read that Napoleon took eight pounds a month, and that Frederick the Great, scorning snuffboxes except as ornaments, would daily fill one of his pockets with snuff!

Be this as it may, smoking was soon thoroughly established in England. The yeoman resting at his plough would smoke a little pipe, its bowl a halved walnut shell, its stem a straw. Some men of fashion would go to the length of carrying pipes made of silver about with them. But the majority of smokers, then as for the next few hundred years, preferred those pipes of fragile white clay that are still occasionally to be seen on sale in the better tobacconists. In 1596, a German traveller, commenting on the theatres and other amusements like bull-baiting and bear-baiting, described how

> [a]t these spectacles, and everywhere else, the English are constantly smoking the Nicotian weed, which in America is called Tobaca—others call it Pætum—and generally in this manner: they have pipes on purpose, made of clay, into the farther end of which they put the herb, so dry that it may be rubbed into powder, and lighting it, they draw the smoke into their mouths, which they puff out again through their nostrils, like funnels, along with it plenty of defluxion and phlegm from the head.[25]

From England, the habit was spread first into Holland and then throughout the rest of Europe.

e: Turkey

Its introduction was made into the Ottoman dominions about the end of the sixteenth century. Since the Portuguese were active in the Turkey trade, as elsewhere, it may have been they who introduced it. But, by whatever route it first entered, its use rapidly increased to the point where later observers would reason that tobacco had not come from America at all, but from the Levant. To this day, some of the best blends come from Turkey and Syria. No atonement could absolve the Turks from the destruction of Byzantium. But their planting of tobacco in Macedonia has given the profligate modern Greeks some reason for not grumbling quite so loudly as they do. By the Turks its use was also spread east, into Persia and the culturally

---

[25] From Paul Hentzner, *Itinerarium*, Nuremberg, 1612—quoted, Compton Mackenzie, *Sublime Tobacco*, Chatto & Windus, London, 1957, p. 88.

dependent areas of central Asia.

f: India

It was undoubtedly the Portuguese who took it to India. The Brahmins at first had certain religious scruples against smoking, since to carry anything to the lips more than once was to risk defiling themselves with a bodily excrement. But they had none against snuffing, and members of the lower castes and the Moslems had no objection at all to smoking. Before very long, the cultivation and export of tobacco were a considerable business. It was actually from India, rather than America, that the cigar was taken to England, our word cheeroot being a corruption of the Tamil *shuruttu*.

g: Japan

By the Portuguese also, it was taken to Japan, where smoking was immediately adopted among every class of subjects, from the geisha girls to workers in the rice fields. The Japanese for "tobacco merchant" appears as early as 1578. By 1607, the city of Hokubu was famous for its blends of tobacco. From Japan it was spread to Korea, for a few years after 1598 a Japanese colony. Tobacco remains Korea's main agricultural export.

h: China

To China it was introduced from several directions. It came from Korea, from the Spanish settlements in the Philippines, and from Portuguese Macao. It quickly spread through the whole of the Empire. The Chinese soon developed their own strains of tobacco, and began making pipes of bamboo, ebony, ivory, the base and precious metals, and even glass. Their glass snuff boxes are still prized items of sale in any auction room. From India and China, tobacco was spread to those parts of the Eurasian land mass to which it had not been already introduced. When the Russians began their vast imperial expansion under Peter II, there were few places where tobacco was unknown.

j: Africa

It was from Portugal, again, that it was first taken to Africa. As early as 1607, the natives of the west coast had been taught its use. Among the Congolese, the very word for smoking, fumu, comes from the Portuguese *fumo*. Into the southern part of the continent tobacco was taken by the Dutch in 1652. The Cape settlers found the soil admirably suited for its cultivation, and they had soon begun a profitable trade with the Hottentots. In north East Africa, the Galles had their tobacco from Europe, but found their own use for it. they neither smoked it nor ground it into snuff. Instead, they would ferment it, strain off the liquid and chew what remained. This they would sometimes improve in flavour by mixing with cow dung.[26]

That the Arabs first learned of tobacco from the Portuguese is recalled by their word for it—*Bortugal.* Its cultivation was already established in Mecca and Medina by 1605. The Egyptians have been regular smokers at least since 1603.

iv: The Use of Tobacco: A Universal Custom

In 1560, the nations of the Old World could be divided into those among which tobacco was used and those among which it was not. By 1660, this division had ceased very largely to exist. In almost no other respect, was humanity yet united in culture. There was no common language. The devout of every religion had little more in common than a mutual bigotry. The Jew ate no pork, the Hindoo no beef. The strict Moslem drank no wine. In Europe, no woman but a whore bared her legs in public. In parts of Africa and America even royalty went about stark naked. In England, bigamy was a hanging offence. The wealthy Turk took pride in his seraglio. The Confucian put all hopes of futurity in the progress of his sons. The Mingrelian killed and ate his sons, and had often previously gelded them to increase their succulence. Certainly, if in varying degree, there were everywhere to be found those necessary protections of property and the lives of those who owned it without which society cannot remain in being. But it was to a very widely varying degree that they were to be found; and, beyond the essential, the range of more or less optional morality differed without end. Yet, within a century, the use

---

[26]Koskowski, *op. cit.*, p. 35.

of tobacco had been spread from the Americas into every part of the world to which the merchants could gain access; and, in spite of every change of fashion and other circumstances since then, tobacco has retained the common regard of mankind. It has done so because nothing else has ever been discovered more exactly suited to the meeting of certain common wants.

v: The Reasons for its Spread

a: Pleasurable Effects

First among these wants are the physical. Tobacco brings enjoyment, or at least relief. For some, it has been known to banish hunger and thirst. For others, it makes eating and drinking more pleasant. It takes the mind off grief. It aids contemplation. It stimulates. It relaxes. One cigarette soothes a smoker's mind in readiness for bed, and another sets him up in the morning. The effects of tobacco depend oddly on what is wanted from it. But, whatever they are, these effects are generally welcomed. It was Sir Compton Mackenzie's opinion that without his continual pipe-smoking, he would not have written half of what he did. Nothing served so well for composing his mind to work. "I would argue" he writes, "that every man, whatever his race, whatever his rank, whatever his profession, whatever his work, is helped by smoking".[27]

Bismarck would have agreed. A cigar, he said,

> acts as a mild sedative without in any way impairing our mental faculties. [It] is a sort of diversion: as the blue smoke curls upward the eye involuntarily follows it; the effect is soothing, one feels better tempered.[28]

---

[27] Mackenzie, *op. cit.*, p. 345. Novelist, essayist, poet, playwright, as well as classical liberal, the author's life (1883-1972) almost exactly spanned the great socialist interruption. But he found consolation in tobacco. He smoked his first cigarette in 1887 and his first whole cigar in 1891; and his rough estimate was that, by the 29th of August, 1956, he had smoked 200,000 pipes of tobacco (*ibid*).

[28] Quoted, Count Egon Corti, *A History of Smoking* (translated from the German by Paul England), George G. Harrap, London, 1931, p. 257.

Napoleon III, whose destruction was Bismarck's greatest and most terrible achievement, would also have agreed. He did much to popularise the cigarette in France, his own consumption of them running to what was then thought the remarkable number of fifty per day.[29] He so entirely lacked his uncle's disregard for the lives of others that he could only bear to watch his battles by chain smoking throughout.

If for a somewhat perverse reason, Wilde might also have agreed. "You must have a cigarette" he has Lord Arthur Wotton say to the painter. "A cigarette is the perfect type of a perfect pleasure. It is exquisite, and it leaves one unsatisfied. What more can one want?".[30]

For Florence King, a cigarette is a "uniquely pleasurable footnote to sex....

> I remember those easy-going smoking sessions with [one of my lovers]: the click of the lighter, the brief orange glow in the darkness, the ashtray between us—spilling sometimes because we laughed so much that the bed shook.[31]

For the modern smoker, there are the medical risks to be borne in mind. But, while very few of us wish to die, there is more to life than the putting off of death. Nor is it certain that a life made miserable by the denial of every possibly dangerous pleasure will be a long one. As Homer had Glaucus address Sarpedon nearly three thousand years ago:

> Oh, my dearest friend, if only, escaped
> from this battle, we could live ageless and
> immortal, neither would I fight in the foremost
> ranks, nor would I send you into

---

[29]*Ibid*, p. 254-5.

[30]Oscar Wilde, *The Picture of Dorian Gray*, New American Library, New York, 1962, p. 93.

[31]Florence King, "I'd Rather Smoke than Kiss", in *National Review*, New York, 9th July 1990.

the struggle that gives men renown. But now
(since ten thousand shapes of death forever
stand about us, and no mortal may flee or
avoid them), let us advance.[32]

And the older smokers often had a different view of the relationship
between tobacco and health.

b: The Alleged Medical Benefits

The American Indians had long believed in its medicinal properties.
It was taken by them as a cure for toothache, frostbite, burns,
venereal ulcerations and rashes, malignant tumours, and much else.
The European doctors showed an immediate interest. It was tried on
a variety of conditions, and belief in its efficacy became, during the
first half of the seventeenth century, quite extravagant. Sometimes,
not all the advertising of the tobacconists could rival the advocacy of
certain medical writers. By one Dr Johannes Vittich it was even
claimed that

> [t]here can be no doubt that tobacco can cleanse all impurities
> and disperse every gross and viscous humour, as we find by
> daily experience. It cures cancer of the breast, open and eating
> sores, scabs and scratches, however poisonous and septic,
> goitre, broken limbs, erysipelas, and many other things. It will
> heal wounds in the arms, legs and other members of the body,
> of however long standing.[33]

---

[32]*Iliad*, xii, 322-328:

ὦ πέπον εἰ μὲν γὰρ πόλεμον περὶ τόνδε φυγόντε
αἰεὶ δὴ μέλλοιμεν ἀγήρω τ᾽ ἀθανάτω τε
ἔσσεσθ᾽, οὔτέ κεν αὐτὸς ἐνὶ πρώτοισι μαχοίμην
οὔτέ κε σὲ στέλλοιμι μάχην ἐς κυδιάνειραν·
νῦν δ᾽ ἔμπης γὰρ κῆρες ἐφεστᾶσιν θανάτοιο
μυρίαι, ἃς οὐκ ἔστι φυγεῖν βροτὸν οὐδ᾽ ὑπαλύξαι,
ἴομεν ἠέ τῳ εὖχος ὀρέξομεν ἠέ τις ἡμῖν.

[33] Quoted in Corti, *op. cit.*, p. 103.

It was lauded particularly as a preventive of the bubonic plague, until the eighteenth century a regular and dreaded visitor to Western Europe. During an outbreak at Nimeguen in 1636, Dr Isbrand van Diemerbroek credited his survival, despite his unfearing devotion to the sick, to his heavy smoking. Once, believing himself overcome by the contagion, he had to hurry home, and believed that he was saved only saved by his promptness in smoking "six or seven pipes of tobacco".[34] Twenty nine years later, the plague made its last and most celebrated appearance in London, where, among a population of just under half a million, it soon killed 70,000.[35] In his diary entry for the 7th of June of that year, Samuel Pepys testifies to the continued belief in tobacco:

> This day, much against my Will, I did in Drury-lane see two or three houses marked with a red cross upon the doors, and "Lord have mercy upon us" writ there=which was a sad sight to me, being the first of that kind that to my remembrance I ever saw. It put me into an ill conception of myself and my smell, so that I was forced to buy some roll-tobacco to smell and to chaw, which took away the apprehension.[36]

It was now that the boys of Eton College were set to smoke a pipe every morning to keep them healthy. One old boy later told Thomas Hearne, the antiquarian, how he had been flogged when found not smoking his ration.[37] Elsewhere in England, tobacco had for some time already been denied, if at all, only to girls. Writing of his travels through England in 1666, Jorévin de Rochefort records how, in the course of a visit to Worcester, his friend

---

[34]*Ibid*, p. 99.

[35]David Ogg, *England in the Reign of Charles II*, Oxford University Press 2nd edition, 1956, Volume One, p. 292.

[36]*The Diary of Samuel Pepys* (Robert Latham and William Matthews, eds.), Bell & Hyman Limited, London, 1972, Volume VI, p. 120. The double hyphen is editorial, to indicate Pepys' own use of hyphenation.

[37]*Ibid*, footnote 2.

asked me if it was the custom in France, as in England, that
when the children went to school, they carried in their satchels,
with their books, a pipe of tobacco, which their mothers took
care to fill early in the morning, it serving them instead of a
breakfast; and that at the accustomed hour every one laid aside
his book to light his pipe, the master smoking with them, and
teaching them how to hold their pipes and draw in the tobacco;
thus accustoming them to it from their youth, believing it
absolutely necessary for a man's health.[38]

Medical attention was not confined to Europe. The Hottentots made
it into powder and applied it as a specific against scorpian bites. The
Chinese used it in the treatment of colds and skin diseases, as well as
of malaria, skin parasites and obesity. Mixed with pine resin, its
inhalation was supposed to remedy a bad circulation.

There were contrary opinions. Hadrianus Falckenburgius, one of the
most famous doctors of the early seventeenth century, was
convinced that tobacco injured the brain. Then there was the general
revulsion of medical opinion as soon as the more extravagant claims
were falsified. It was soon evident that tobacco did not set broken
bones, or clear away skin rashes, or cure cancer, or prevent the plague.
The doctors had fallen into a simple but common error. They had
observed what was evident—that the immediate effects of tobacco
were often to raise a patient's spirits; and these, even today, can do as
much for recovery as the most powerful drug. Given a little optimism,
and the utter lack of any statistical method as corrective, they went
straight to their conclusion, that it could cure everything.

But this revulsion had its limits. Tobacco was seen as far less valuable,
but was retained in the pharmacopoeia. Indeed, as recently as 1901, it
was still suggested on good authority as a treatment for respiratory
disorders. 39 39. And its retention may have had good reason.

---

[38]Quoted, Mackenzie, *op. cit.*, pp 157-8.

[39] W. Hale-White, *Textbook of Pharmacology and Therapeutics*, Pentland Young,
Edinburgh—cited in Ben Whittaker, *The Global Fix: the Crisis of Drug Addiction*,
Methuen, London, 1988, p. 146.

Tobacco appears to aid digestion, and to loosen the more intractable deposits of mucous. Its calming effect on the mind is shared by various organs of the body; and there are those who suggest that a little smoking might help in the avoidance of ulcers and other conditions related to stress.[40] Even today, with all that we have learned, or been taught to believe, it may be that tobacco is less an uncompromising enemy of the human body than an ambiguous and often costly friend.

c: The Social Benefits

It owed some part of its spread to the advice of the doctors. But its continued popularity derived from other causes. Its physical attractions alone would have guaranteed it a place. Consequent on these, though, were its social attractions. Wherever tobacco has been introduced, it has rapidly become indispensable to most kinds of gathering.

The Indian peace pipe has become a cinematic *cliché*. Whether those who smoked it were always as faithful to their bond as the romantic anthropologists would have us believe may be doubted.[41] But the value, where dealings with strangers are concerned, of a shared activity that relaxes without dulling the mind is obvious. It is the ideal aid to diplomacy; and cigarettes have been a moderating force in every kind of negotiation, from wage bargaining in the Midlands to the settling of disputes along the line dividing free from socialist Korea.

It has an equal value in the making of personal friends. There are few

---

[40] See, for example, David Loshak, "A Whiff of Consolation for the Smoker", in *The Daily Telegraph*, London, 30th October 1981; or the Late T.E. Utley, "Lighting up for Liberty", in *The Times*, London, 3rd August 1987.

[41] See, for example, Cornelia H. Dam: "[T]he act of smoking, even on ordinary occasions, [was] a pledge of mutual confidence among the Indians as taking salt together is among the Arabs, and the pledge of the peace pipe was seldom broken by individuals or tribes until the white man came to teach the Indian the material advantages of perfidy", (Tobacco among the Indians, in *The American Mercury*, XVI.61, January 1929, p. 76).

places where someone can sit down among perfect strangers and at once join in the conversation. In England, for sure, this sort of pushing in is firmly discouraged. Without an introduction, most people tend to ignore each other. Words are exchanged, if at all, for a plainly limited purpose. Anything beyond this is met with suspicion. Smoking is the traditional means here of breaking through this reserve. See, for an early example, Joseph Addison:

> I was Yesterday in a Coffee-House not far from the Royal Exchange, where I observed three Persons in close Conference over a Pipe of Tobacco; upon which, having filled one for my own Use, I lighted it at the little Wax Candle that stood before them; and after having thrown in two or three Whiffs amongst them, sat down and made one of the Company. I need not tell my Reader, that lighting a Man's Pipe at the same Candle, is looked upon among Brother-smoakers as an Overture to Conversation and Friendship.[42]

Nearly three centuries later, tobacco has much the same function. Imagine: Two strangers sit opposite in an otherwise empty railway carriage. After a long silence, one clears his throat and makes a desultory comment—on the weather perhaps, or some matter concerning the journey. An answer is made not deterring all further communication. A cigarette case is taken out and presented. The cost of one cigarette, even with the immense weight of the taxes heaped now on it, is small, though its value as a gift may be considerable. Not merely is a common activity joined, but friendship is offered. If accepted, the conversation can begin. It may have left one open to the attentions of a bore for the rest of the journey. It may have been the prelude to a life-long attachment. More likely, it will simply have enabled the passing of a few hours more pleasantly than a silent counting of telegraph poles would have allowed. If Englishmen smoked less, they are continually told—and told most often at their own unwilling expense—they would live longer. Beyond any doubt, they would also make fewer friends.

---

[42]Joseph Addison, Richard Steele *et al.*, *The Spectator*, No. 568, Friday, July 16, 1714, "Everyman" Edition, London, 1966, Volume Four, p. 287.

Yet if tobacco can be used to dissolve barriers, it can also be used to reinforce them. By restricting their access to it, the inferior status of certain groups can be more sharply defined. It is not only the anti–smokers in the modern West who support the laws against the supply of tobacco products to children; nor were these laws themselves invariably enacted in response to the medical panic of the past four decades. Alternatively, an exclusion may be founded on some difference in the method of using tobacco.

One such difference can be seen to have emerged in England after 1660. Before then, smoking—or, to a much smaller extent, quid-chewing—had been common to almost everyone who used tobacco, irrespective of wealth, status or opinion. The men who faced each other in the Parliament of 1641, and who subsequently faced each other on the battlefields of Naseby and Edge-Hill, were divided on nearly every fine point of constitutional and religious doctrine. They wore different clothes, and caroused in different fashions. They gave their children very different names. But, when they called for tobacco, it was from clay pipes of the same design that they smoked it. The Cavaliers who returned with Charles II, however, had passed at least a while in French exile, and had brought back to England an enthusiasm for France. During the next thirty years, Whitehall became in every respect—and many of them were thoroughly shameful—a satellite of Versailles, as did, to a lesser extent, London become one of Paris. Along with periwigs, moral laxity, a taste for rhymed drama, and all else by which the new courtiers and their clients set themselves apart from the rest of the nation, was snuff. Smoking was seen as the act of a provincial or a Puritan, never of a gentleman. Macaulay describes the most fashionable coffee houses of the period:

> The atmosphere was like that of a perfumer's shop. Tobacco in any other form than that of richly scented snuff was held in abomination. If any clown, ignorant of the usages of the house, called for a pipe, the sneers of the whole assembly and the short answers of the waiters soon convinced him that he had

better go somewhere else.[43]

In turn, snuffing was seen as the act of a cold-hearted, sensual fop, with a hatred of the old Constitution and a taste for Roman Catholicism.

The Glorious Revolution put an end both to Royal absolutism and all attempts at a Counter-Reformation in England. But the distinction between those who smoked and those who snuffed remained throughout the eighteenth century. The coffee house described by Addison was filled with members of the commercial classes or the minor gentry. No one who pretended to any higher station would have willingly sat smoking in public. Edward Gibbon was the grandson of a City merchant, and, before the publication of his immortal History gave him a measure of independence, he earned much of his living from public sinecures given him in exchange for his vote in Parliament. Even so, he claimed descent from the same stock as the Hapsburgs, and his Swiss exile had left him with tastes more French than English. Accordingly, he took snuff. He would arrive in company dressed in such ornate splendour as almost to divert attention from the great hanging hydrocele that was one day to kill him, and would make his jewelled snuff box into a solid punctuation of his discourse. Three loud raps with the fingers of his right hand would indicate that he had something to say that he considered of more than usual force and elegance. Sometimes, he would pause, with a flourish carry a pinch of the best snuff to each nostril, and then continue. It is easy, leaving aside his genius, to see Gibbon as a caricature of the eighteenth century man. But caricature is often no more than exaggeration; and, so far as the use of tobacco is concerned, it was only in the late nineteenth century, with the introduction of the cheap cigar and, at last, of the cigarette, that the English returned to a form of use common to all classes.

---

[43]Thomas Babington Macaulay, *History of England from the Accession of James II*, (1849-61), Everyman Books, J.M. Dent, London, 1910, Vol. 1, p. 285 (Chapter III).

d: Religious Uses

Tobacco, said Thomas Corneille, is divine: it has no compare.[44] Not surprisingly, in view of the plant's real and apparent qualities, this has often been taken as literally true. The American Indians familiar with its use believed without exception in its divine origin;[45] and its ritual use appears to be as old as its discovery. Among the Mayans, it was regularly offered to the gods both as incense burned on the altars and as smoke from the mouths of the worshippers. One of the best preserved reliefs from their ancient temple at Palenque shows a priest smoking a cigarette. Among the Aztecs, it was a necessary accompaniment to the ceremonies at which thousands of captives were slain in sacrifice to the god Tezcatlipoca. The medicine men of the more primitive Tonoupinambaultiis tribe in Brazil would fill and light their pipes and puff the smoke into the faces of the assembled laity, the purpose of this being to transmit the heroic virtues. "The warriors, thus prepared, attacked their enemies with demoniac fury and almost inevitably were victorious".[46]

Similar notions were formed quite independently in the Old World. At Dahomey, in West Africa, the dignitaries attending the rites of human sacrifice formerly held there would each be assigned servants decorated with imitation tobacco leaves; and the King, as principal smoker, would puff smoke into the mouths of his guests. Among the Hottentots, as soon as a boy was born, he would have a cigar put in his mouth, while his mother bit off and ate his right testicle. This was considered a very beneficial operation, giving the child, among other qualities, fleetness of foot.[47] In parts of Asia also, tobacco had, and

---

[44]   *Quoy qu'en dise Aristote, et sa digne Cabale,*
        Le Tabac est divin, il n'est rien qui l'égal...

Lines from his *Le Festin de Pierre* of 1677, a versification of Molière's *Don Juan*—Corti, *op. cit.*, p. 179 and illustration facing p. 188.

[45]See *supra*, footnote 21.

[46]Koskowski, *op. cit.*, p. 70.

[47]*Ibid.* In support of this last, Koskowski cites B. Laufer, W.D. Hambly and R.

sometimes still has, a religious significance.

But, in Christian Europe, it had none. While its divinity was proclaimed by the younger Corneille, he should be seen as making no more than a poetical flourish—as following a convention according to which every beloved was a goddess and every military patron a hero. Even if his own regard for tobacco did extend to its worship, a settled body of opinion within the Church of which he was formally a member was in opposition to its use. It may seem strange, or perhaps monstrous, to relate: but there were occasions when the persecution of tobacco was advocated, and actually carried into effect, on the grounds of religion.

IV: The Persecution of Tobacco—Part One

i: Spanish America

Coming from the religious authorities in Spanish America, the earliest opposition, while hardly justified, was sufficiently explained by the reasons given for it. The conversion of the natives went ahead for the most part without any use, or even threat, of force. No matter how great the secular crimes committed, there was in America no equivalent of the religious oppression that accompanied the reconquest of Spain from the Arabs. But, if, bearing in mind their faith and the age in which they lived, the missionaries were not extreme bigots, one conviction they had brought from home. They believed the signs of a true conversion to be not only adherence to the doctrines of their Church, and observance of its ceremonies, but also a complete giving up of any practice that seemed—no matter how indifferent in itself it was—at all associated with the old faith. In Spain, the converted Jews and Moslems were spied on to see how many more baths they took than their longer established brothers and sisters in Christ. In America, bearing in mind all that was seen by the missionaries, it was impossible at first not to make an association of tobacco with paganism. When the Indians came into church, then,

Linton. *Tobacco and Its Use in Africa*, Field Museum of Natural History, Chicago, 1930.

smoking for all the world as if they were at a pagan ceremony, they met with the most severe disapproval.

In 1575, a Mexican ecclesiastical council forbade the use of tobacco in any church throughout Spanish America. However, the prohibition was so ineffective that even some priests had soon taken to its use. No amount of propaganda could hold them from realising that an easy distinction could be drawn between the religious and the other uses of tobacco.[48] In time, the distinction was to be made by everyone, as paganism was either forgotten or concealed in the main centres of population; and the religious opposition lapsed. But, before this was to happen, the penalties against tobacco were increased. By a decree of the Provincial Council convened at Lima in 1588, its use was forbidden to any priest, under pain of eternal damnation, while at the altar. A year later, the Council of Mexico declared that

> [o]ut of regard for the reverence due to the Holy Eucharist, it is hereby commanded that no tobacco in any form whatever be taken by clerics before reciting Holy Mass, or by any person before receiving Holy Communion.[49]

ii: Europe

Yet, while the American prohibitions are sufficiently explained by the circumstances in which they were imposed, it is difficult to see why, on purely religious grounds, they were imitated in Europe. There

---

[48]For the regret of a priest who was unable to distinguish, see a letter home of 1550 from one father Nobrega: "All the food is difficult to digest, but God has remedied this with a plant, the smoke of which is in much aid of digestion and for other bodily ills and to drive out moisture from the stomach. No one of our brothers uses it, nor does any other of the Christians, in order not to imitate the unbelievers who like it very much. I need it because of the dampness and my catarrh, but I abstain—not what is useful for myself [do I want] but what is good for many that they might be saved" (quoted in "The Social Role of Smoking", in Robert D. Tollinson (ed.), *Smoking and Society: Towards a More Balanced Assessment*, D.C. Heath, Lexington, Mass., 1986, p. 170).

[49] Issued, 27th October, 1589—quoted in Corti, *op. cit.*, p. 107.

never was any general prohibition; but local action was sometimes taken. In Seville, for example, by 1642, some of the clergy at Seville had become habitual smokers and snuffers during the celebration of the Mass. In that year, following complaints, Pope Urban VIII issued a Bull forbidding the use of tobacco in any church throughout the diocese, the penalty for infringement being immediate excommunication. His successor, Innocent X, issued a similar Bull in 1650 to cover the Church of St Peter in Rome.

iii: A Theological Excursus

Why were these Bulls issued? The association of what is present with was is inconceivably distant is harder made than when both are present; and, so far as I can tell, no one ever claimed that a man who took up smoking in Spain or Italy was just as likely to pick up a flint knife and start a cult of the great god Tezcatlipoca.

iv: The Bible

Nor, this excuse removed, is there any direct condemnation to be found in the *Bible*. There are statements against wine that can be extended to cover tobacco. According to Paul, for example, drunkards shall not inherit the Kingdom of God.[50] But this and all other such claims have seldom been construed as sanctioning a prohibition of alcohol, but merely as against against immoderate indulgence. It is, moreover, open to doubt whether tobacco is in the same class of substances as alcohol.[51] There are various schools of exegesis by using the methods of which any text can be made to give any desired meaning, from predictions of when the world will end to injunctions for or against Apartheid. Doubtless, by the same methods, the most damning attacks imaginable on tobacco could be extracted. But in the way of this stands common sense, together with a suspicion—which, admittedly, is no proof—that, whatever else it might be, the *Bible* is not a book of crossword puzzles.

---

[50] *1 Cor*, 6:9-10.

[51] On this point, and on some of the following, see my *The Right to Smoke: A Christian View*, Chapter 2 in this work.

Undeniably, tobacco was seen as a pollutant. But it was not seen as one in the most usual modern sense of the word. The two Papal Bulls against its use in church did stress its dirty effects. People were sneezing and even spitting on the floor. Smoke was staining the altar linen and endangering sacred works of art. Yet, while spitting may be a vile habit, it was no more insanitary than the frequent exposure and burial of corpses in church. The burning of incense creates as much smoke as tobacco, and the greasy deposits of the past five centuries have damaged or destroyed some of the best Renaissance frescoes. Moreover, the same dislike was shown by many of those Protestants for whom a church was very much less a place of ritual and adornment. Tobacco was seen as a pollutant in church less because it was dirty than because its use was seen as unnatural.

v: The Law of Nature

Following the vague notion, first held by the Greeks, that "the good" corresponds in some degree to what is found outside of human custom, objections to tobacco have frequently been grounded on its being contrary to nature. But, on any candid examination of the matter, this grounding must be seen as of a quite illusory solidity. In the first place, the concept of nature appears to have been almost unknown—or, at least, ignored—by the primitive Christians. Christ made no use of it. Paul makes a single unambiguous reference to it, and then not to prove more than a very trivial point.[52] Peter's use of it is actually derogatory: "But these, as natural brute beasts, made to be taken and destroyed, speak evil of the things that they understand not; and shall utterly perish in their own corruption".[53] Here, godliness is contrasted with the call of nature, not identified with it. The construction παρα τον της φυσεως νομον[54]—against the law of

---

[52] *1 Cor*, 11:14—"Doth not even nature itself teach you, that, if a man have long hair, it is a shame unto him?" ἢ οὐδὲ αὐτὴ ἡ φύσις διδάσκει ὑμᾶς ὅτι ἀνὴρ μὲν ἐὰν κομᾷ, ἀτιμία αὐτῷ ἐστι.

[53] *2 Peter*, 2:12 ὡς ἄλογα ζῷα φυσικὰ γεγεννημένα εἰς ἅλωσιν καὶ φθοράν).

[54] The phrase is taken from Clement of Alexandria—*his Pædagogus*, 3.3.

nature—is nowhere to be found in the *New Testament*. The concept of nature as a criterion of right conduct was fully introduced only by the educated Greek converts of the second century; and it was made a full and harmonious part of Christian theology only by the scholastic philosophers of the twelfth century. Therefore, by those Protestants who regard systematic thought as a hindrance—or, perhaps, as an alternative—rather than a help, to understanding the Word of God as revealed in the *Bible*, the words "natural" and "unnatural" are never safely to be used. Any Protestant who gives utterance to the claim that "if God had wanted us to smoke, he would have put chimneys out of our heads" is making a potentially dangerous concession to the Scarlet Whore of Babylon.

In the second place, while Roman Catholics need have no fear of using these words, the problem, where smoking is concerned, is to give them a definite meaning. Can it be said that, by subordinating his rational faculty to a desire for corporeal pleasure, the smoker is rejecting the nature given him by God? If tobacco were like alcohol, the answer might be yes. The normal tendency of habitual and immoderate drinking is to destroy both mind and body. The effect of nicotine is simply to alter their states in various, comparatively mild, ways. Nor, unlike alcohol, does it create a will-rotting addiction. Some smokers there have always been for whom giving up has been a painful effort. Yet this typically involves a depression and a certain irritability which reaches its greatest intensity within a day or so of stopping, and then steadily reduces. The craving can last for years. But there is nothing about the physiological effects here comparable with the hallucinations and convulsions that some alcoholics feel on drying out. These are facts so evidently true from experience, that I can scarcely conceive how anyone with eyes and a brain could honestly dispute them.

Nor can it consistently be said that smoking represents an unnatural use of a bodily function. In 1653, a committee of Saxon bishops and university professors issued a manifesto in which we read that

> [i]t is both godless and unseemly that the mouth of man, which
> is the means of entrance and exit for the immortal soul, that
> mouth which is intended to breathe in the fresh air and to utter

the praises of the Most High, should be defiled by the indrawing and expelling of tobacco smoke.[55]

Smoking does put the lungs to a novel and unexpected use. But, while, if we are Darwinians, we can say that the lungs did not evolve for this use, if we are creationists—as most Christians were before the last century—who are we to say what use God had in mind for any of our organs, back in the late October of 4004 BC, when he created the heavens and the earth out of nothing? Considered in itself, smoking is neither more nor less an abuse of our nature than is shaving the hair off parts of our body or clipping a pair of spectacles to the bridge of the nose.

The obvious answer here would be to refer to the medical evidence. Whether or not we choose to regard all of the claims against tobacco as true, or even as likely, we are easily able to distinguish the lighting of a cigarette from the wearing of spectacles. But what we can do is currently of no importance. The question is on what grounds the men of the sixteenth and seventeenth centuries could distinguish the use of tobacco from any number of other non-natural yet accepted activities. And, bearing in mind what medical evidence they had before them, they had no such grounds whatever.

vi: The Likeliest Reason

When hostility to any act or substance is based on grounds that plainly, or according to the knowledge available, do not support it, the likeliest explanation is that the stated grounds are false. The denunciations against tobacco, though most frequently couched in theological terms, do not follow either from any commonsensical reading of the Bible, or from any consistent train of scholastical reasoning. In all likelihood, they follow instead from two propositions. The first is that novelty is to be distrusted. Even with so much reason as we, in the West, have to despise this worst kind of conservatism, we sometimes give way to it. Over our ancestors, it had a much wider dominion. When smoking had just been introduced

---

[55]Ibid, p. 115—quoting from H. Piltz, "Über den Tabak und das Rauchen", Leipzig, 1899, p. 148.

into England, one story goes, Sir Walter Raleigh was sitting at home, enjoying a quiet pipe. A gardener came into the room, thought his master on fire, and poured a bucket of water over him. Less happily, another story records how Rodrigo de Jerez—who, it may be recalled, was perhaps the first European to smoke tobacco—went back to his home town, where he so alarmed his neighbours with the clouds of smoke coming from his mouth, that they denounced him to the Inquisition, and had him locked away. He remained a prisoner for some years; and, on being set free, found that everyone else had taken to smoking.[56]

The second proposition is that whatever is enjoyed by others, and not by oneself, is wrong. This dislike of other people's pleasure has never lain entirely dormant in any generation; and it has in some been let out of all control. To the extent that tobacco gives pleasure to its user, it has always attracted the hatred of those puritan bigots who, as Macaulay so memorably taunted, "hated bearbaiting not because it gave pain to the bear, but because it gave pleasure to the spectators.[57] The sixteenth and seventeenth centuries were the ages in which the puritans of every sect were at their most powerful. It seems only likely that, having begun to hate tobacco for reasons that they could hardly announce to the public—or, indeed, honestly to themselves—they should have snatched at any denunciation on theological grounds, and not been too concerned about giving it any proper justification.

V: The Persecution of Tobacco—Part Two

It may seem that I have given far too much space to seeking to explain the religious prohibitions in Europe. They were always limited in nature and extent. They were never strictly enforced. Yet, while in themselves limited, they did set an example and provide excuses for the much more important attacks on tobacco mounted by some governments.

---

[56]Corti, *op. cit.*, p. 50.

[57]Macaulay, *History*, op. *cit*, vol. 1, p. 129 (Chapter III).

i: Germany

The most important attacks within Christendom came in the Holy Roman Empire, that loose confederation of states, nominally or actually under Hapsburg control, which now roughly comprise Germany, Czechoslovakia and northern Italy. The Thirty Years War, ending in 1648, though disastrous, had settled the military debate on the Reformation. The individual states of the Empire might still persecute dissenters within their own jurisdictions; but the formula *cuius regio eius religio*—whose the territory, his the established faith—had left the crusading zealots of both sides frustrated. It is probably no coincidence that the cry against tobacco went up within a few years of the War's ending.

Nothing could exactly replace the thrill of religious controversy. But, being both new and popular, this was a good substitute enemy. Pens that had formerly written for or against the Real Presence and Predestination continued the same hysterical outpouring of ink, but in another direction. The most famous of these diverted controversialists was Jakob Baldé, a Jesuit, whose writings reveal him as a something between the Juvenal and the David Simpson of his age. Take, as examples, the following passages:

> So soon as a ship with tobacco from overseas comes into port—they can scarce wait till the stinking cargo is unloaded—they take the first boat they can find, and off they go to the vessel. Then a box must be opened and a sample of tobacco cut off from the roll, that they may taste the nasty stuff, into which they stick their teeth as greedily as if it were the daintiest of morsels. If they find it to their liking, then they are all athirst to enjoy it, and quite beside themselves with happiness. After some gaping they begin to bargain and inquire the price; ducats or golden guineas, 'tis all one to them—they grudge no expense for an article like this: what is the good of money, they say, if it is to lie idle in the purse? Money, we all know, is more precious than virtue, but unto them tobacco is dearer still....

> What difference is there between a smoker and a suicide, except that the one takes longer to kill himself than the other?

> Because of this perpetual smoking, the pure oil of the lamp of
> life dries up and disappears, and the fair flame of life itself
> flickers out and goes out all because of this barbarous habit.[58]

The authorities were often of the same mind. In Cologne, as early as
1649, the Archbishop—who was also the political
sovereign—decreed a general prohibition of the "sale and purchase
and use of tobacco everywhere, under penalty of incurring Our high
displeasure and punishment, together with the confiscation of the
tobacco and the pipes". [59] The punishment was a fine or
imprisonment, the severity of each increasing with a repetition of the
offence. One of the reasons given in the decree was the risk of fire. In
those days of closely built, timber houses, before the emergence
either of household insurance or of efficient fire fighting services,
this was a dangerous risk, and goes some way, it must be granted, to
the dislike of tobacco. But, while smoking might understandably be
legislated against, neither snuffing nor quid-chewing could have
involved any threat of fire. I might also say, in passing, that the
prohibition covered the medical use of tobacco. What kind of
concern does a government show for its subjects when it bars them
from a substance that—however falsely—they believe to be a
valuable medicine?

In 1652, the Electors of Bavaria and Saxony issued general
prohibitions. That same year, they were joined by the Moravian Diet.
Within a few years, much of the Empire was covered at least by
restrictions on smoking or the other uses of tobacco, where not by
prohibitions. Until 1691, in Luneburg, smoking even carried the
death penalty.

Needless to say, these had no large effect—save, perhaps, to bring
the law into disrepute by reason of its perversion to immoral and
unattainable ends. In 1662 a proclamation to the Bohemians

---

[58] From his *Die Truckene Trunkenheit* (Drunk without Drinking), Nuremberg,
1658—quoted, Corti, *op. cit.*, p. 119.

[59] *Ibid*, p. 110.

complained how, in spite of all efforts as suppressing it, tobacco was now smoked by everyone—even in the streets. "The common people" it stated

> are so given up to the abuse that they imagine they cannot live without several pipes of tobacco a day—thus squandering in these necessitous times the pennies that they need for their daily bread.[60]

ii: Switzerland

A similar experience was had those parts of Switzerland where Calvinism held sway. Inspired by this gloomy—and, in many respects, scandalous—doctrine, the authorities proceeded against tobacco with the same ferocity as they brought to their other interferences in what should have been matters of private choice. After the first laws had utterly failed, more severe ones were tried. In Zurich, for example, in 1667, it was decided by the Burgomaster and Council that offenders should be set to work on the city walls. If they were caught again, they would be beaten with rods, or branded, or exiled. In Berne, a table of police regulations based on the Ten Commandments was drawn up, and smoking was included in the prohibition of adultery. In 1675, an institution known as the Tobacco Chamber, and modelled on the Roman Inquisition, was founded, its purpose being to track down and punish all uses of tobacco. But these laws were just as complete a failure as the first. The Swiss were too fond of their tobacco. Some of them, moreover, were beginning to make large sums by trading in it. The authorities in Basle, which had become home to an international market in tobacco, refused all commands and persuasions to interfere in the trade.

iii: Russia

The government of Russia, then, as always, was less restrained than its Western counterparts in ensuring obedience to its will. The Orthodox clergy there took against tobacco for much the same

---

[60]*Ibid*, p. 116.

reasons as the Roman Church. But, ignorant of Augustine and Aquinas—and, for that matter, of all speculative theology—they preferred to base their opposition on the text: "The things which come out of him, those are they that defile the man".[61] They had a firm ally in Michael Feodorovich, the first Romanov Czar. His reign, from 1613, to 1645, was an age of fierce persecution for all users of tobacco, smokers or otherwise. He declared its use a deadly sin, and forbade possession for any purpose. A Tobacco Court was established to try breaches of the law. Its usual punishments were slitting of the lips, or a terrible, and sometimes deadly, flogging with the knout. Occasionally, offenders were castrated; or, if they were rich, they were exiled to Siberia, and their property was confiscated.

iv: Turkey

But the most extreme persecution took place in the Ottoman Empire. Though still at the height of its power, though still able, indeed, as late as 1683, to have an army lay siege to Vienna, the Empire was in decline. The stern, but limited, authoritarianism that had allowed the Turks to conquer the whole southern and eastern rim of the Mediterranean, from Casablanca to Baghdad, from Budapest to Aswan, had given way to the worst form of oriental despotism. Each new Sultan emerged from a seraglio intrigue. He secured his power by a massacre of his brothers. His exercise of power was restrained neither by any institution nor by custom. He ruled his capital through a cabal of eunuchs and favourites, and the provinces through governors answerable to him alone. In spite of this, there were Sultans of distinction, and even greatness, whose efforts did much to ensure the Empire's survival into the present century. But there were also Sultans who might, in every particular, have stepped out of the pages of Suetonius and Tacitus. Murad IV, who ruled between 1623 and 1640, was a Sultan of this latter kind. Among the particular objects of his tyranny was tobacco.

Since Mohammed died nearly a thousand years before the European discovery of America, the *Koran* is as silent as the *Bible* on tobacco.

---

[61]*Mark*, 6:15.

Like the Bible, it does cry out against alcohol: "Intoxicants and gambling... are an abomination—of Satan's handiwork: eschew such abominations that ye may prosper".[62] But there have always been doubts as to whether these prohibitions extend to tobacco. As with Christianity, Islam has been heavily influenced in its philosophic theology by Aristotelianism; and no one who has read Aquinas will find the works of Al-Ghazali or his followers at all strange in their fundamentals. But, again, no conception of the natural and unnatural has ever been made that would allow a consistent attack on smoking or any other use of tobacco. The most extremely devout Moslems certainly condemn it, as they condemn all pleasures that are not immediately joined with the contemplation of God. But, such extremes of devotion, while always respected, have never been more common in Islam than in other religions. The general opinion today throughout the Islamic world is that the use of tobacco is neither un-Koranic nor unnatural. Even the Saudi Wahabbites, the strictest sect of Islam, no longer regard smoking as a criminal offence.

In the seventeenth century, when tobacco was still a novelty, opinion was more evenly balanced. Yet, while the theologians tended to regard the prohibition of wine as applying to all mood-altering substances in general, it was hardly out of piety that the Sultan took against smoking. Contravening the explicit Word of God, he was a furious drinker, and it was a complication of gout brought on by his drinking that eventually caused his death. He probably hated tobacco for the same reasons as the puritans in Europe hated it—because it gave others a pleasure that he did not himself know, or that he did not wish to know.

It is said, though not on unanimous authority, that laws against smoking had been made during the previous reigns, and that punishment for their breach involved the offender's having a pipe-stem thrust through his nose, and his parading through the streets of Constantinople on a donkey. Murad, however, applied himself to the putting down of smoking with a thoroughness and brutal severity unique in history. As with Nero, his immediate excuse

---

[62]*Koran*, Sura., V, verse 93.

for persecution was a fire.

On the 7th of August, 1633, while the capital was celebrating the birth of his son with general, and prudent, rejoicing, a firework landed on a ship at anchor in the Golden Horn and set it afire. The flames spread to the dock and then to the city. Before the fire was brought under control, it had razed 20,000 wooden buildings. Since fire fighting was a government enterprise, and the officials in charge of it had behaved with gross incompetence, there was an outcry. Men would come together in the coffee houses and complain to each other over a pipe of tobacco. Since, suspicious even of his own spies, Murad was in the habit of going about Constantinople in disguise, to find out for himself what was being said against him, Murad was soon aware of this. He accordingly put out a decree, announcing that the fire had been caused by the smokers, and ordering that all places where smokers were known to gather should be demolished.

This decree was soon followed by another, in which smoking was prohibited on pain of death. Adding the role of policeman, judge and executioner to that of spy, he continued his secret visits. His pleasure was to accost a suspected tobacco dealer and beg him to sell a small quantity, offering a price outrageous even compared with those obtaining on the black market. If the dealer's caution was overcome by greed, and he produced a bag of tobacco, Murad would behead him on the spot. His body would lie in the street, an example of the imperial justice. Invariably, his estate would be confiscated.

Wherever the Sultan went, the number of executions would rise. Even on the battlefield, he would make a point of seeking out smokers, and punishing them by beheading, hanging, cutting in quarters, or crushing their extremities and leaving them helpless between the lines. No one knows how many suffered from this disgraceful law, though, by the time of his death, at the age of twenty nine, Murad had put to death well over 100,000 of his subjects—a quarter of them during his last five years. This may seem a very small total to us, who are used now to reckoning the victims of tyranny in millions and tens of millions. But, for a man who lacked the gas chamber and the machine gun—and whose whims never went to the full madness of telling farmers how to grow food—100,000 is a very respectable figure for a reign of seventeen years.

For all his efforts at enforcement, though, Murad's laws were as complete a failure as those in Europe were later in the century. The Turks and the subject peoples of the Empire continued to smoke. The laws were repealed in 1648 by Mohammed IV—himself a smoker—and were not repeated.

v: Japan

Not every prohibition, however, was made on the grounds of religion. Ignorant both of Jewish monotheism and of Greek philosophy, when, in 1609, the Japanese *Shôgun* forbade the cultivation and use of tobacco for any purpose, his stated intention was simply to keep the peace. In that year, the Bramble and the Leather Breeches smoking clubs had been formed in the old capital city of Kyoto. Their members—chiefly young nobles—were to be recognised by the enormously long and heavy pipes that they had either to wear strapped round their waists like swords, or have carried behind them by retainers. Their chief delight was to go about, provoking street brawls. After an outcry, the clubs were dissolved; and since, as frequently happens, disapproval of what was pernicious was extended to cover what was only accidentally connected with it, smoking was prohibited.

While the clubs were suppressed, the prohibition as it applied to tobacco was ignored. Either the authorities still failed to distinguish smoking from disorder, or the public order was only an excuse for attacking tobacco. For, in 1612, it was further decreed, that the property of anyone taken in the act of selling tobacco should be given to his accuser. In 1616, the penalties were made yet more severe. But all was to no effect. Before long, the very princes who had made the laws were breaking them. Tobacco was quietly absorbed into Japanese tradition; and a pipe soon accompanied the cup of tea ceremonially offered to a guest in polite society. The laws against it were all repealed in 1624. There was a feeble effort to revive them during a few years after 1695. But this never amounted to more than a petty vexation. The Japanese remain among the heaviest smokers in the world; and their low incidence of lung cancer is a standing embarrassment to the anti-smoking hysterics of our own day.[63]

vi: England

Nor was the opposition in England primarily religious. As with the rest of the nation, tobacco was too popular among the clergy for there to be any serious question of seeking its prohibition as ungodly. What opposition there was came largely from one man. What it was about tobacco that James I hated is unknown. Mackenzie suggests that the whole passion was a cover for his virulent hatred of Sir Walter Raleigh.[64] Probably, he just disliked the thought of all that pleasure derived from it by others. But, whatever his reason, it was his great misfortune that he should have hated tobacco as bitterly as did his contemporary fellow ruler, Murad of Turkey. For he was quite unable to suppress it.

The Tudors had made a great show of their absolutism; and their nationalisation of the English Church, so removing any alternative source of authority within the Kingdom, had made them on paper the most powerful monarchs in Christian Europe. But their power was almost entirely a *facade*. On the Continent, the growth of standing armies during the sixteenth century had everywhere destroyed, or seriously weakened, the constitutions that had once limited the royal power. In England, this development had been delayed until its effects elsewhere had become evident, and will and reason had been found to oppose it. Philip of Spain, whose theoretical power over his subjects was shared with the Pope, could raise taxes on the stroke of a pen, and grind down any person or institution that dared resist him. Elizabeth of England stood uniquely between her subjects and God, but had no armed force wholly under her command but her palace guard; and for money she had to apply to a Parliament that she could influence but never control. Her power was a *facade*, kept intact by her own personality and by the affectionate conniving of her subjects.

---

[63]On this point, see H.J. Eysenck, "Smoking and Health", Tollinson, *op. cit.*, pp 32-7.

[64]Mackenzie, *op. cit.*, p. 102.

James, her nephew and successor, came down from Scotland, in 1603, believing that he really had inherited a position of unlimited power—that he really was to be regarded, as the more Courtly divines were daily preaching, as God's vice-gerant on Earth. He soon discovered the true state of affairs in England. He had no force of personality, and his subjects, as soon as they had his measure, began openly to despise him. He was Scottish. He was deformed. He stank. He slobbered. He was a passive homosexual who enriched his lovers at the public expense. Undoubtedly, he was learned. But, where Elizabeth's learning had sat easily on her, his took the form of a querulous pedantry that moved those round him to laughter. Even his one great service to his people, the peace with Spain, was condemned by the standards of the day as cowardice. His entire reign was taken up with a quarrel over money, that was eventually to merge with a quarrel over the meaning of his title. He wanted open access to the wealth of England. The House of Commons resisted him at every attempt. When it came to an attack on tobacco, he had no better weapons at hand than a propaganda campaign and what few fiscal and regulatory powers had not yet been removed from his dwindling prerogative.

His first work of propaganda dates from within a few months of his accession. Writing in Latin,[65] he laments how England was fallen from her old glory. Formerly, her sons had been brave in war and obedient in peace to the authorities. Now, the clergy were grown lax, the nobility sunk in idleness, and the people as a whole suffering a steep moral decline. the only answer was a reform from above, which would begin by abolishing the all-corrupting weed. Since these arguments had no observable effect, James made his next attempt in English.

Published anonymously in 1604—it was only publicly acknowledged in 1616—*A Counterblaste to Tobacco* repeats but also elaborates the earlier pamphlet. Smoking is condemned as a new custom learned

---

[65]*Misocapnus Sive de Abusu Tobacci Lusus Regius* (Smoke-Hatred, or a Kingly Sport on the Use of Tobacco), London, 1603. I have never seen a copy of this pamphlet, but am following the summary given by Corti, *op. cit.*, pp 76-7.

from barbarians. Its medical benefits are denied. Rather, it is, in the strongest terms alleged to be harmful: it is addictive; it "makes a kitchen... oftentimes in the inward parts of men, soiling and infecting them, with an unctuous and oily Soote as hath bene found in some great Tobacco takers, that after their death were opened".[66] Finally, comes the famous peroration to the English people:

> Have you not reason then to bee ashamed, and to forbeare this filthie noveltie, so basely grounded, so foolishly received and so grossly mistaken in the right use thereof? In your abuse thereof sinning against God, harming yourselves in person and in goods, and taking also thereby the markes and notes of vanitie upon you: by the custome thereof making your selves to be wondered at by all forraine civil Nations, and by all strangers that come among you, to be scorned and contemned. A custome lothsome to the eye, hateful to the Nose, harmefull to the braine, dangerous to the Lungs, and the blacke stinking fume thereof, neerest resembling the horrible Stigian smoke of the pit that is bottomeless.[67]

The cries of a few flatterers aside, the answer to this Royal question was a firm "no". The English continued to smoke. And so the King tried supplementing persuasion with force. By a Proclamation dated the 17th of October, 1604, he raised the import duty payable on tobacco by exactly two thousand percent—from 2d to 6/8d the pound. But, while, looked at one paper, this was a fierce increase, it had little more practical effect than the pamphlets. The tax was evaded by smuggling and by home cultivation. Had James been allowed his way in all else, he might have continued his fiscal attack. As it was, however, he was compelled by circumstances to suspend it.

vii: Tobacco Turns to Gold

After their first years of poverty, certain of the English settlers in North America realised that there was money to be had from

---

[66]*A Counterblaste to Tobacco* (1604), Rodale Press, London, 1954, p. 32.

[67]*Ibid*, p. 36.

growing tobacco for export. The first known shipment to England was made in 1613, but was ill-received, the *Nicotiana rustica* that was native to Virginia being decidedly inferior to the *tabacum* that was to be had from the Spanish plantations. But, with the replacement of the poorer with the better strain, the conquest of the English market rapidly began. In 1616-7, Virginia sent 2,300 pounds to London, compared with 58,300 Spanish pounds. Within two years, Virginia was sending more than 20,000 pounds.[68] In 1620, 40,000 pounds were imported.[69] As the trade increased, the colonists made both mercantile and political allies in England; and effort was soon diverted from the suppression of all tobacco to the promotion of Virginian tobacco at the expense of foreign.

At the same time, James continued in need of money. It was now discovered how easy it was to tax imported tobacco, and what immense sums could be raised from it. In 1608, he lowered the duty to one shilling, entrusting its collection to one of his lovers. In 1615, he made the import of tobacco into a Royal monopoly—in open breach of the law as decisively stated in 1602—and farmed it out for a yearly rent of £14,000. In 1619, he tightened the monopoly by prohibiting the cultivation of tobacco around London. The following year, he extended the prohibition to the whole of England, so starting a war that still continues, if with abatements, between State and citizen over the right to grow the herb of one's choice in his own back garden.

If with greater moderation, Charles I shared his father's detestation of tobacco; and he would have none of his courtiers use it in his presence. But he also was too short of money to pick and choose its source. He continued the monopoly. To this, in 1633, he added the licensing of retailers. He and James both railed against the allegedly addictive nature of tobacco. Yet, while, in all succeeding reigns, there have been innumerable subjects able to give up its use for various reasons, no British Government has ever found the will to do

---

[68]Mackenzie, *op. cit.*, p. 110.

[69]Corti, *op. cit.*, p. 92.

without the revenue raised from it.

During the eighteenth century, indeed, not even the frequent wars with France were suffered to disrupt the trade. From its small beginnings, American tobacco had long since acquired the predominance on the world market that it still justly holds. The French conceived so passionate a fondness for it that they quite neglected to develop their own plantations in Louisiana and Martinique. The British Government feared that, in the event of a wartime embargo, the French would, however reluctantly, shift the balance of their purchases, so diminishing its revenue and inviting the resentment of the wealthy and influential tobacco interest. The French Government had no wish to compound its disastrous record in the wars with England by depriving its subjects of their favourite tobacco. Therefore, an agreement was reached. By special licence, the trade would continue in time of war, the ships involved in it leaving from a named port in Great Britain to a named port in France, carrying only tobacco and returning empty.[70] It was in part the prospect of open access to Virginia that had the French take the side of the revolted American colonists: and the close naval blockade of France during the revolutionary and Napoleonic wars—during which more desperate struggles the old agreements were not renewed—pressed never so hard as in its limiting the availability of

---

[70]Mackenzie, *op. cit.*, pp 213-4, gives an example, dated the 3rd of June, 1756, of the firm of licence issued:

> Upon application made to His Majesty in Council, a Pass hath been ordered to be forthwith issued under the Great Seal for the following ship to export Tobacco to France, in like manner as was done during the last war with France. The Marion of Glasgow, British Built, Burthen one hundred and fifty tons or thereabouts, carrying Twelve men, Alexander Morrison, Master, Laden with two hundred hogsheads of Tobacco, to sail from Glasgow to Bourdeux in France.

> I am ordered to acquaint you with this information of the Commissioners of His Majesty's Customs, that the necessary directions may be given to the proper officers at the Port of Glasgow from whence the ship is to sail.

American tobacco.

It was the realisation generally that tobacco could, in spite of all doubts on other grounds, be made an ever-flowing fountain of money that brought its persecutions to a halt. The various German prohibitions were scarcely sooner shown to have failed than they removed and taxes imposed in their place. In Bohemia, within three years of the complaint, mentioned above, about the popular disobedience of the laws against tobacco, the trade was made legal and subject to tax. In 1669, the Elector of Bavaria, financially embarrassed, called the Diet into session and agreed a tax on tobacco, the decree of 1652 being withdrawn. In 1670, the Emperor himself was brought round to the creation of a State monopoly. Soon after his accession, in 1689, Peter the Great of Russia repealed all the prohibitions, associating snuffing and smoking—both learned from the West—with modernity. In 1697, for a down payment of £13,000, he sold a monopoly of its importation and sale to an English stock company.

VI: The Persecution of Tobacco—Part Three

It may seem strange that the only serious persecution of modern times took place in the United States. Not only have the Americans their enviable written Constitution and Bill of Rights, both designed for the restraint of improper authority, but, as said already, their southern states grow and export some of the finest tobacco in the world. Yet they also have always had among them a large and well-organised puritan minority; and, during the second half of the last century, this minority conceived a wild aversion, first to cigarettes, and then to all tobacco.

Introduced in its modern form from abroad, the cigarette came late to the United States. Even so, it rapidly established itself as the main form of tobacco use, largely displacing both quid-chewing and the pipe. In 1865, less than 20 million cigarettes were produced. By 1880, this figure had risen to 500 million. Another five years, and it had risen to 1 billion. Another five years, and it had doubled, to 2 billion.

By 1895, 4 billion cigarettes were produced.[71]

The reason for this growth was that cigarettes were both cheap and convenient. For this reason they gave offence to the puritans. First, rumours were spread. It was claimed that the papers were saturated with opium and arsenic, that the tobacco was reused from old cigar butts picked off the street, or that it was urinated on to give it flavour. Accusations of effeminacy were made. "The cigarette is designed for boys and women" said The New York Times in 1884.

> [T]he decadence of Spain began when the Spaniards adopted cigarettes, and if this pernicious practice obtains among adult Americans, the ruin of the Republic is at hand.[72]

Alternatively, it was claimed that boys were turning to cigarettes. Our own anti–smokers are not the first to realise what may be achieved by playing on the supposed threat to children posed by tobacco. The country was swamped with lying or exaggerated propaganda on this theme. Children would go colour blind, it was said, if they smoked cigarettes. They would go bald. Their growth would be stunted. They would go insane. They would be sterile. They would be impotent. They would become sexually promiscuous. They would become moral degenerates. "Many and many a bright lad" said Charles Hubbell, a New York school commissioner in the 1890s

> has had his will power weakened, his moral principle sapped, his nervous system wrecked, and his whole life spoiled before he is seventeen years old by the detested cigarette. The 'cigarette fiend' in time becomes a liar and a thief. He will commit petty thefts to get money to feed his insatiable appetite for nicotine. He lies to his parents, his teachers, and his best friends. He neglects his studies and, narcotized by nicotine, sits at his desk half stupefied, his desire for work, his ambition,

---

[71]Gordon L. Dillow, "The Hundred-Year War Against the Cigarette", reprinted from the February/March 1981 issue of *American Heritage* by The Tobacco Institute, Washington D.C., p. 6.

[72]*Ibid*, p. 7.

dulled if not dead.[73]

By 1901, Louisiana and Wyoming were the only States left in the Union not to have passed laws restricting the sale and public consumption of cigarettes. In some States, both were prohibited. In the Indiana legislature, a bill had been introduced that, if passed, would have subjected public smokers to imprisonment and a fine, together with disfranchisement and incapacity to hold any office of trust or profit. In Chicago, a special clinic was opened, for the "cure" of smokers; and hundreds of the repentant guilty queued to have their palates painted with silver nitrate solution. When a touring opera company visited Kansas, it shifted the first act of *Carmen* from outside a cigarette factory to outside a dairy. The campaigners were so confident, so contemptuous of the basic rules according to which a free society must operate, that, when the Supreme Court of Illinois struck down a State law against the sale of cigarettes, they actually began a campaign to abolish the independence of the judiciary.

But the American anti–smokers failed. They never obtained a federal prohibition. Without this, it was almost impossible to enforce the State laws. The Constitutional bar to restrictions on interstate commerce allowed a large mail order business to grow and flourish. In some States, the laws were so loosely drafted that they were repealed by human ingenuity: matches were sold at 10¢ the box, with a packet of cigarettes given free. While the number produced fell at first—as low as two billion in 1901—it soon returned to its spectacular climb, reaching nearly eight billion by 1910.[74] Moreover, once the early claims about the effects of smoking on health had been tested and falsified, the laws began, one after the other, to be repealed. Even where not repealed, they fell largely into disuse. By the American entry into the Great War, in 1917, it was considered almost natural that the troops sent to France should be assigned their daily packet of cigarettes. By 1928, the number of cigarettes

---

[73]*Ibid.*

[74]*Ibid*, p. 12.

produced in the United States reached 100 billion.[75]

But what really turned the puritan attack in America was the success of the campaign against alcohol. This had involved much the same people who denounced the cigarette, but had been vastly more impassioned. There had been decades of propaganda. Temperance preachers had gone from town to town, dipping worms in glasses of beer, then taking them out dead, to show the supposed effect of alcohol on the human body. Songs were composed and taught to the children. As early as 1851, the State of Maine had made the sale of alcoholic drinks illegal but for medical reasons. At last, in 1919, the Eighteenth Amendment to the Constitution was ratified, allowing a Federal prohibition. "The reign of tears is over" said the popular evangelist, Billy Sunday on the passage, in 1920, of the Volstead Act that imposed the prohibition. "The slums will soon only be a memory. We will turn our prisons into factories and our jails into storehouses and corncribs. Men will walk upright now, women will smile, and the children will laugh. Hell will be forever for rent".[76]

For a while, it was supposed that, if drink could be made illegal, it might be just as possible to secure a Nineteenth Amendment against the other great enemy of the pleasure-hating bigots of America. "Prohibition is won, now for tobacco" said Billy Sunday.[77] But the prohibition was unenforceable. Too many people had too strong a taste for drink ever to be kept away from it. Smuggling and illegal home production both rose spectacularly and every effort to prevent them was a failure. Within ten years, more than half a million Americans had been arrested for some violation of the anti-alcohol

---

[75]*Ibid*, p. 14. Compare this, however, with the 695 billion produced in 1978—p. 6. Many of these were for export rather than home consumption. But the sheer inconceivable number stands as tribute to the productive power of the American economy.

[76]Quoted by Milton Friedman, *An Economist's Protest: Columns in Political Economy*, Thomas Horton, New Jersey, 1972, p. 160.

[77] *Ibid.*

laws. Another 35,000 had died from alcoholic poisoning.[78] The laws were repealed in 1933. But, for thirteen years, criminals had been allowed to take over the running of a great and profitable industry. The effects of this, on the organisation of crime and on public honesty, have never been reversed. A lesson partly learned, for the next forty years, tobacco would be left alone.

VII: The Modern Prospect

By 1930, tobacco seemed, seemed, to at least one well-informed observer, to have finally triumphed. "[A] glance at the statistics" declared Count Corti,

> proves convincingly that the [non-smokers] are but a feeble and ever-dwindling minority.[79] The hopeless nature of their struggle becomes plain when we remember that all countries, whatever their form of government, now encourage and facilitate the passion for smoking in every conceivable way, merely for the sake of the revenue which it produces....

> In European countries, no serious attempt to prohibit smoking has been made in recent times. Though it is possible to enforce the drink laws in the United States by means of a gigantic organisation, any proposal to deal in the same way with smoking would call forth such a storm of disapproval as would instantly sweep any government out of office that attempted it,

---

[78]Whittaker, *op. cit.*, p. 137.

[79]He gives the following table—which I abbreviate—for average numbers per head of population:

Country	Cigars Smoked Per Head		Cigarettes Smoked Per Head	
	Pre-1914	1927	Pre-1914	1927
Germany	119	103	195	502
England	12	4	201	811
France	16	10	96	248
Holland	---	157	---	341
Italy	34	39	104	372
Sweden	38	33	115	233
USA	90	62	143	840

and the same may be confidently affirmed of every country in the world. If we consider how in the past the efforts of the most absolute despots the world has ever seen were powerless to stop the spread of smoking we may rest assured that any such attempts to day, when the habit has grown to such gigantic dimensions, can result only in a miserable fiasco.[80]

Evidently, Corti had anticipated neither the antipathy of the National Socialists nor the medical discoveries, or claims, of the next sixty years. So far from a dwindling minority, the non-smokers are now a growing majority of at least the British and American populations. Yet, tempting as it might be to dismiss his conclusion as disproved by later events, Corti's main point—that smoking and the other main uses of tobacco are too securely entrenched to be easily dislodged—is probably as good today as when it was made. It may be, as the anti–smokers implicitly assume, that users of tobacco are made rather than born; and that, given continued hectoring, the number can be reduced eventually to zero. More likely, if I draw the right lesson from history, many, or most, of them are drawn to it by some requirement of their nature. Neither the threat of Hell-fire, made by the American Church, nor the threat of earthly torments, made and actually carried out, by Murad IV, could entirely hold tobacco and its users apart. Nor, if ever tried, will the more sanitised, though also better policed, persecutions desired by Action on Smoking and Health have any greater success.

Yet, for all these considerations, it remains, now as throughout the past three centuries, that the surest protection of tobacco is not the propensity of the governed to resist, but the insatiable need of the governors for money. During the fiscal year 1987-8, the British Government raised £5,775 million in excise duty and value added tax from the sale of tobacco products.[81] This gigantic sum is equivalent to half the hospital bill to the National Health Service, or one fifth of the defence budget. It is also greater than the national income of

---

[80]*Ibid*, pp 265-7.

[81]Written answer, *Hansard*, 19th December 1988, p. 28.

most black African countries. To suppose that, without a reduction of its spending that would be unique in living memory, any likely government would do without this source of revenue is inconceivable. And, to suppose that, having made the necessary reductions, one would not be prevented, by its political and economic ideology, from coming between its subjects and their preferences is equally inconceivable.

"There is no stopping us" says David Simpson. We shall see.

2. THE RIGHT TO SMOKE:
A CHRISTIAN VIEW

If the trumpet give an uncertain sound, who shall prepare himself to the battle? (1 Cor., 14:8)

Introduction

I do not wish to deny that there are health hazards associated with smoking—just as there are health hazards associated with virtually all activities people find pleasurable, from drinking to jogging.

Around two fifths of the adult British population do smoke. This has been a declining fraction of the whole during the past thirty five years, or ever since the first hard evidence of the likely risks to health were published. In 1970, 128 million cigarettes were smoked here. By 1984, this figure had fallen by 22 per cent, to 99 million.[82] 99 million cigarettes, even so is still enough laid end to end to stretch between New York and Babylon. Two fifths of the adult population is still around 18 million people.

Not surprisingly, then, smoking and tobacco are a public issue of considerable importance. Its importance has grown in recent years with each new revelation of the dangers involved. Some part of this, to be sure, has to do with the possibility that non-smokers might be at risk from inhaling the allegedly carcinogenic fumes of others' cigarettes. But, in the absence of anything approaching definite proof, talk of 'passive smoking' must be thought for the moment of secondary value. Easily the largest part of the issue concerns the degree to which smokers should be allowed to harm themselves. What debate, therefore, is currently taking place may be seen as a specific skirmish in a more general struggle. This struggle is between the advocates of authority and the advocates of freedom. On the one side, there are the British Medical Association, representing the doctors, and the small pressure group, Action on Smoking and Health, representing itself. These want, if not the outright

---

[82] M. A. Plant, *Drugs in Perspective*, Hodder & Stoughton, London, 1987, p. 66.

prohibition of tobacco, then certainly very severe restrictions on its consumption. This involves, at the least, tight controls on the advertising of tobacco products, and progressively heavier taxation of them. Their propaganda ranges from the solidly factual to the absurd. Sometimes pictures are handed round, showing the effect of tar on the average pair of lungs. Occasionally, someone like the anti-smoking expert, M. A. H. Russell, goes about proclaiming such arrant nonsense as that "[o]nly about 15 per cent of those who have more than one cigarette avoid becoming regular smokers."[83] On the other side is an as yet loose coalition of committed smokers and libertarians. The interest of these first is evident. They enjoy their habit, and resent any threat to their right to go on doing so. The members of the second may or may not themselves enjoy smoking. What moves them is a passionate belief that no one should be forced to do what others regard as in his or her best interest. Following John Stuart Mill, they assert that "[o]ver himself, over his own body and mind, the individual is sovereign."[84]

As yet, the political parties are largely unaligned in the debate. True, the Labour Party inclines to the anti-smoking lobby. It is on record as having proposed bans on cigarette advertising save at the point of sale,[85] and on the placing of cigarette vending machines.[86] But the Conservatives cannot be regarded as inclining to the other side. It was Sir George Young, then a junior health minister in the first Thatcher Government who said in 1980 that "[t]he traditional role of politicians has been to prevent an individual causing harm to another, but to allow him to do harm to himself. However, as modern society has made us all more interdependent, this attitude is now

---

[83] M.A.H. Russell in 1971, quoted in Heather Ashton & Rob Stepney, *Smoking: Psychology and Pharmacology*, Tavistock Publications, London, 1983, p. 140.

[84] John Stuart Mill, *On Liberty* (1859), Everyman Books, J. M. Dent., London, 1977, p. 73.

[85] *The Times*, London 3rd April 1986.

[86] *The Times*, London, 12th July 1986.

changing."[87] Young was moved elsewhere very shortly after. But the Government still spends about 3.5 million per year on anti-smoking campaigns. It still pressures the tobacco companies into further 'voluntary' restrictions on their advertising and promotion. My own suspicion is that its continuing tolerance of the industry owes less to the ideas of J. S. Mill than to the £5,000 million or thereabouts raised each year from taxes on tobacco products.

This is, however, beside my current point. What I propose here to discuss is whether there can be any specifically Christian view of the matters raised above. There are Christians who also have decided views on smoking. A couple of years ago, for example, what the newspapers described as "two hundred church and community groups" joined in calling on the Government for a significant increase in tobacco duties.[88] Again, it would be incredible if, of the eighteen million Britons who smoke, none was additionally a devout churchgoer. But, in both these cases—and especially in the former, judging from its context—the taking of sides in the argument has not been connected with any fundamental point of theology. Rather, it has been an instance of what Edward Norman calls the "politicization" of religion.[89] It shows the adoption by churchmen of whatever political ideology may currently be the general fashion, and its being given a religious gloss subsequently. Arguments purely over the extent of individual harm or the nature of individual rights in society are secular matters. They can have no validity to a Christian, deliberating as such, unless they can be first connected with some precept of the Divine Law. Before any answer can be attempted, our proper objects of enquiry must be stated. These are: whether

---

[87] Quoted in Ashton and Stepney, *op. cit.*, p. 144.

[88] *The Times*, London. 27th January 1986.

[89] Edward Norman, *Christianity and the World Order* (being the BBC Reith Lectures for 1978), Oxford University Press, 1979, p. 2. I do not, in this essay, adopt Dr Norman's position, which is that there is no political ideology inherent in the doctrines of Christianity. But I do admire the force and clarity with which he exposes the pretensions of today's political clerics.

smoking tobacco is contrary to this Law, and, if so, whether there is any implied right or obligation to use the coercive power of the State against smokers. Since these are largely subsumed in the wider question, of what scheme of human politics is most compatible with the Divine Law, this also ought to be examined. But first to be discussed is smoking as a matter in isolation. With this I shall begin—though not until I have dealt with a number of preliminary issues which I feel it my duty not to avoid. For, addressing myself as I am to an audience which is, at least in part, hostile or indifferent to Christianity, I must first answer the inevitable question in reply to my own—of whether it matters what God is supposed to think about smoking; or, more generally, of what religion has, in the modern world, to do with politics and morality. Many atheists do ask this, and seem to think it a clever question. It has two answers.

I: Religion, Politics and Morality

The first is simple and obvious. Sacred and secular matters always have been connected in the popular mind, and probably always will be. And, sad though perhaps it is to mention, the history of Christianity has been, to an extent uncommon even with religion, a history of persecution. Its first legal recognition came in the year 313, with the Edict of Constantine. This was a grant of toleration, on a basis of complete equality with every other faith in the Roman Empire. It was not enough. The Christians were a minority, but they had the Imperial family as converts. Their bishops were both able and eager to influence the direction of State policy in religious affairs. Eighty three years later came the Edict of Theodosius, suppressing the Pagan ceremonies. The performance of rites which had come down in unbroken sequence since before the time of Homer, and which formed the agreed basis of classical civilisation, was made a capital offence: and the laws were rigorously enforced. It was not until the year 529 that the Athenian schools of philosophy were closed by the Emperor Justinian. But Paganism by then had been effectively dead for generations. Its wiping out remains a very impressive achievement.

Then there were the heretics—or those rival Christians who in any doctrinal argument had the weakest force of arms. Few people seem greatly worried today whether Christ is *homoousios* or *homoiousios*; whether his substance is identical to that of the Father, or merely similar to it. Those Christians in the fourth century who spoke only Latin were somewhat perplexed, since the two Greek words both translated as *consubstantialis*. But, in the eastern half of the Empire, it was a question of the highest importance. Street mobs fought pitched battles over its correct resolution. Bishops kicked each other to death. So far from its eventual subsiding, further questions came to depend on it. If Christ were *homoousios*, had he two natures, or one, or two and one? If he had the two and one, might he still have only one directing will? The Arian and Monophysite and Monothelite controversies together continued during more than three centuries, blasting the lives and happiness of millions.

As a regular issue, heresy became prominent in Western Christianity only with the revival of learning. But the struggle, when it came, was even more frantic than it had been in the east. One of the minor controversies in early Byzantium had concerned whether the body of Christ were incorruptible. In early modern Europe, the greatest one concerned whether, or to what extent, it might be edible. The wars of religion, fought ostensibly to settle this point, lasted more than a century, ending only in 1648. The internal persecutions died out only in the century following this. The point had not been settled. What happened was that the educated classes for the most part found other interests. Toleration was, at first, the child not of agreement, nor of mutual charity, but of indifference.

An obvious reply to this, of course, is that the spirit of persecution is now almost entirely alien to Christianity. So, in doctrinal matters, it is. To a Catholic, Protestants are no longer damnable heretics. Since the Second Vatican Council, it has been felt more appropriate to call them "separated brethren". Few Protestant leaders have appeared unwilling lately to be photographed beside the Pope. No respectable divine now blames the Jews for having killed Christ. Moslems and Hindus are invited to ecumenical services, and are even welcomed when they occasionally turn up. This flabby syncretism may have done much for the public order. It has certainly been carried to an extent embarrassing to the more thoughtful Christians. If He can be approached by other paths, which are equally valid, why should God have sent His only begotten Son to be scourged half to death and then nailed to a cross? If the Hindu can have a thousand gods, what was so bad about the Classical Pantheon? Doctrinal persecution is certainly alien to the larger of the modern churches. But this kind of it is only the more noticeable—because, since the Enlightenment, the more shocking—half of what Christianity has been taken as standing for.

The general case for persecution was most clearly stated by Ambrose, Archbishop of Milan in the fourth century. To have—or to be able to acquire—the means of suppressing what is abominable to God, and not to use them, he told the Emperor, is to partake of its guilt.[90] Evidently, this applies in any dispute as to the nature of Christ. It applies equally with regard to observing his moral teachings, apparent or inferred. Following from this second conclusion, politics, already subordinated to religion, becomes wholly fused with it. For example, in the Pagan Empire, divorce was easy; suicide carried little reproach; homosexuality was variously honoured or ignored. Each is said to be a sin. In Christian Europe, each was at least discouraged by law. And, if they have explicitly rejected the first conclusion, most Christians continue to argue and behave as though they still accepted the second. Few seem willing to disclaim the right to impose their moral code on others. Perhaps the Hierarchy in Catholic Ireland might never dream of trying to hold an *auto da fé* in Phoenix Park. It has, nevertheless, opposed every effort made to legalise birth control. The Church of England hires its buildings out for every purpose, from revivalist baptisms to Rastafarian pot parties. Some of its ministers have even tried giving religious sanctuary to a Trotskyite atheist. When the question arose, of letting the shops open on Sundays, it took up the full jargon of the Oxford Movement, and proclaimed England still to be a "Christian country".

If, then, a Christian of the above kind could be persuaded that smoking were in some respect sinful, he would be logically obliged to

---

[90] See Edward Gibbon, *History of the Decline and Fall of the Roman Empire* (1776-87), Everyman Books, J. M. Dent, London, 1962, vol. 3, p. 119 (or, in any edition, the first paragraph of chapter XXVII).

advocate measures against it. He would be obliged to become more extremely and fanatically intolerant on the issue than Action on Smoking and Health and the British Medical Association combined. The secular case against tobacco is that it leads to illness. More or less its grimmest claim is that 'patients who ultimately die from chronic bronchitis or emphysema usually endure about ten years of distressing breathlessness before they die'.[91] This is sad. What is it, though, compared with the sufferings of the damned—in that place 'where their worm dieth not, and the fire is not quenched'?[92] This is what may lie in wait, either for the sinful smoker, or for the undutiful brother in Christ who left him unsupported in his weakness.

II: Is Smoking Sinful?

Anyone finding this unlikely might care to note that smoking actually has in the past been regarded as sinful. In the seventeenth century, Catholics were threatened with excommunication if caught pipe in hand. In Calvin's Geneva, it was not only banned, but the ban was placed among the Ten Commandments. The secular arm gave its usual support. German smokers faced the death penalty until the end of the century. In France, Louis XIII, though not so drastic, still tried forbidding the use of tobacco except by medical prescription.

If smoking really were a sin, and the advocacy of persecution were a requirement of the Faith, then persecution is what the true believer must, in all conscience, advocate. And this is one reason why our present enquiry is an entirely proper one. It might tell the non-believer what to expect should Christianity ever become less languidly militant than it admittedly now for the most part is, even in those matters on which it continues to claim a special authority. Or it might furnish him with useful arguments. But, as justifications go, it is highly contingent. Ten or twenty years ago, when religion seemed on the whole to be a declining force in human affairs, it would have

---

[91] Warning made in 1971 by the Royal College of Physicians; quoted Whitaker, *op. cit.*, p. 147.

[92] *Mark*, 9:44 (repeated 9:46).

been less useful than it is today, when the reverse may be true. In ten or twenty years time, it may be of no account whatever, or of burning importance.

The second justification is not at all contingent for the average non-believer. He may laugh at religion. He may give deliberate offence to others, by calling it a superstitious frenzy or a device for keeping people quiet. Even so, his entire philosophical outlook requires a religious foundation. This religion need not absolutely be Christianity. But it must be something very similar to it. For, without God, there is no morality. I could try supporting this simply by giving a short history of the present century. Christ had more than trees in mind when saying "by their fruits ye shall know them".[93] But I will adopt a more rigorous proof.

III: The Nature of Morality

Whatever I feel I know directly. What you feel I can know only by guessing from your outward appearance. Given sufficient power of will, you could hide your last agony from me. Even made aware of this, I should feel only sympathy for you. This is a sentiment stronger in some of us than in others; and it depends in all of us on the attending circumstances. Imagine, then, that I am bigger than you, and have lured you to a place where I feel secure of there being no witnesses. Assuming that the act, or its consequences, gave me enough pleasure to overbear whatever feelings of sympathy I might harbour, state one reason why I should not cut your throat.

You might say that it would be wrong. But this is no final answer. I ask what is meant by the words 'right' and 'wrong'. Broadly speaking, there are in secular moral philosophy two modes of justifying the use of these words.

According to the first, they are terms of shorthand, applied to actions or rules of conduct, in so far as these are believed useful to the welfare—however this be defined—of a certain group. To the main sort of utilitarian, my cutting your throat, leaving aside any distress

---

[93] *Matt.*, 8:20.

caused to you, might serve as a precedent to other acts of murder. Indeed it might. It might also be that if life and property were held in less general respect than they are, there would be much less of both. Were the common good my standard for measuring conduct, killing you would certainly be wrong. I am not talking generally, though, but about me. If it should stand between me and what I want, I see no reason for not ignoring the common good. You might tell me that doing so is in my 'real' interest; that my setting a bad example raises my own chances of being murdered. None of this touches me. I am the best judge of what is good for me. If I compare all the advantages, present and remote, of killing you, with the small chance that the finding of your body might encourage some stranger to knock me on the head, and they remain positive, I still see no reason to put the knife away. As a theory of what the laws should be, utilitarianism is wonderfully convincing. For an individual's moral obligation to obey them, it gives no basis whatever.

You might turn, then, to the second of the two modes. According to this, right and wrong are the opposing extremes on a scale of values, the existence of which latter may be deduced from observing the order and harmony of the material world. Every existing thing is said to have its own natural function. The function of man is to live as a rational being. In other words, my harming you would be a breach of the 'natural law', and a violation of your rights under it. I could as easily quote Aristotle or Aquinas on this point. Instead, I go to Ayn Rand: 'Rights are conditions of existence required by man's nature for his proper survival. If man is to live on earth, it is right for him to use his mind, it is right to work for his own values and to keep the product of his work. If life on earth is his purpose, he has a right to live as a rational being: nature forbids him the irrational.'[94] If you could harangue me on this lofty theme, for long enough, and with enough eloquence, you might, perhaps, make my heart bleed, and thereby have me put the knife away. But you might do this just as well by describing the tears of an imaginary wife and a few children.

---

[94] Ayn Rand, *Atlas Shrugged*, Random House, New York, 1957, quoted in Ayn Rand *et al.*, *Capitalism: The Unknown Ideal*, New American Library, New York, 1967, p. 323 (her italics).

Utilitarian arguments are valid, even if less widely than those putting them often claim. This sort of natural rights argument is simply absurd.

In the first place, since Rand was an atheist, the words natural law as used by her are meaningless. They are what Roscelin is said to have called a *flatus uocis*—or, to translate him crudely, a verbal fart. A law can be one of two things. It can be a command, to disobeying which a penalty is attached. It can be a statement of what is seen invariably to happen. The words 'if a man lie with a beast, he shall surely be put to death: and ye shall slay the beast'[95] constitute a law. The words 'a projectile having an escape velocity of less than seven miles per second cannot be sent beyond this planet's gravitational field' constitute a law. The words 'cutting my throat would be a violation of natural law' constitute ten words. I expect no punishment if I kill you. I expect no difficulty in killing you.

In the second place, the whole natural law tradition, atheist or religious, is based on a defective epistemology. It begins with Aristotle. He claimed not only that "the beginning of our knowledge lies in the senses", but also that what we perceive with them is an objectively existent reality. To the left of my word processor keyboard, I see a cup of coffee. Let me confirm this with a few basic tests, and, in Aristotelian terms, I have reason to believe that this object exists, and will continue in existence whether I look away, or leave the room, or drop dead.[96] Following this view of sensory perception, Aquinas went so far as to assert that, while the highest knowledge comes from God alone, "there are some truths which the natural reason also is able to reach, such as that God exists."[97] Ayn

---

[95] *Lev.*, 20:15.

[96] Aristotle, *Metaphysics* I, 1, and *Posterior Analytics* II, 15, *et passim*.

[97] Thomas Aquinas, *Summa Contra Gentiles*, Lib. I, cap. iii. All translations from this work are my own. Those from the *Summa Theologiæ* are either compared with those of the Dominican Fathers or are followed entirely. As for this rationalist claim, it is still formally upheld by the Roman Catholic Church. See Heinrich Joseph Dominicus Denzinger: "If anyone shall deny that the one and true God our creator and Lord can be known through the creation by the natural light of

Rand, though she never formulated anything so brilliant as the five empirical 'proofs' by which Aquinas sought to show this, was no less ambitious. From her belief in an objectively existent reality, she claimed to derive an objectively binding moral theory.[98] While arriving at radically different conclusions, the Marxists begin with the same presumption. To them, at least some people are able to know what reality is. Nearly every other rationalist scheme is similarly based.

Yet it should be obvious that no conclusion is ever more secure than the premises on which it rests. Imagine that I land on a desert island and, coming across a bone, say "I think this may be part of a human skeleton. Therefore civilised men once lived here". My argument would be invalid. For the same reason, so are those of the rational moralists. To see this as clearly as possible, let us state the premises of their argument. These are that we perceive things as they really are, and that we use our reason to understand their nature. Let us take them in reverse order.

What allows us to make sense of the external world is the notion of cause and effect. Believing that event A is the cause of event B is our means of explaining or predicting the one from observing the other. I wake and measure the temperature outside. It is five degrees Centigrade. I see a thick frost on the ground that was not there the previous night. I believe the cause of frost to be sub-zero temperatures. Therefore, the temperature in the intervening time has been lower than it is now. Likewise, I measure the outside temperature at midnight. It is minus five degrees. I anticipate frost in the morning. Everyone uses this kind of reasoning. Yet it has itself no rational basis.

---

human reason let him be anathema." (*Enchiridion Symbolorum Definitionum et Declarationum de Rebus Fidei et Morum* (1873), 31st edition, Herder, Freiburg, 1960, Cap. 1806

[98] For the clearest and longest development of Rand's epistemology, see David Kelley, *The Evidence of the Senses: A Realist Theory of Perception*, Louisiana State University Press, 1986.

I paraphrase David Hume. One billiard ball that is in motion strikes another that is at rest. The first loses its motion. The second acquires one. If we examine these events, we reach three conclusions. First, they occur in a particular order of time. One ball is in motion before the collision, the other one after it. Second, the balls touch for their changes of behaviour to occur. Third, if we recall every previous like situation known to us, events have always proceeded in a like manner. Beyond this, we see nothing else. When we talk about the communication of force, we are not describing anything that we have seen, but only a collision of billiard balls. Nor are we stating a logical necessity. Anyone never having seen such a collision, or anything analogous to it, could just as easily imagine the two balls stopping or bouncing back from each other. Force is an inference from the constant conjunction of these events, not an explanation of it. If we predict their continued subsequent juncture, we are assuming that the future will be like the past—an assumption which, by its nature, we cannot prove. I now quote Hume: "[T]here is nothing in any object, consider'd in itself, which can afford us a reason for drawing a conclusion beyond it; ... even after the observation of the frequent or constant conjunction of objects, we have no reason to draw any inference concerning any object beyond those of which we have had experience."[99] What inferences we do draw are the product of an habitual association of ideas, rather than the conclusions of our reason.

This said on the relationship of objects to each other, I turn to their existence. I think again about my cup of coffee. What do I know about it? If I wish, I can make myself see a pattern of colours. I can feel a warm, smooth solidity. I can smell something. I can taste a pleasant bitterness. At no point do I ever perceive a cup of coffee. I experience sensations of one. This is not playing with words. Sensations are separable from objects, and, so, are not necessarily dependent on them. When asleep, I have known very satisfactory cups of coffee without one ever having been 'really there'. It is easily conceivable that the whole universe is no less a figment of my

---

[99] David Hume, *A Treatise of Human Nature* (1739), Book I, Part III, section xii.

imagination. If a sceptic never acts on this doubt, it is because the habit of believing in reality was securely fixed before he could begin reasoning about it.

Finally, there is the matter of whether the self can be proven to exist. It might be thought, following Déscartes, that the assertion "I think, therefore I am" is "so certain and so assured that all the most extravagant suppositions brought forward by the sceptics were incapable of shaking it." The syllogism cannot be false. If it were, I should be mistaken; and, to be mistaken, I must still exist.[100] That it is true I can scarcely deny. But it is only true at the moment of its conception. I exist now. I have no proof that I existed yesterday. In the film *Blade Runner*, one of the characters believes that she is a real person, and that she has memories extending back about thirty years. In fact, she is an android, at most a few months old. The memories were programmed in by her maker. I have no assurance that I am any different; that, when I woke this morning, I had not just been brought into being complete with memories of a past existence. For that matter, I have no assurance that I was not brought into being an hour ago, or five minutes ago, or one second ago—or at any moment prior to the one of which I am immediately aware. Memory can be tampered with. Also, the future is entirely unknown and unknowable. I have no more certainty that I shall still exist then than that I existed in the past. In just what 'the present' consists no one understands. It may be an irreducible but definite particle of time. It may be an infinitely fine division between past and future. In either case, rational knowledge of personal existence is far less certain than it may at first seem.

IV: The Limits of Reason and Scepticism

"Which of you" said Christ, "by taking thought can add one cubit unto his stature?"[101] Which of us indeed? For all the claims made on

---

[100] René Descartes—*Discours sur la Méthode* (1637), part four. See also Augustine (354-430)—*De Ciuitate Dei*, Lib. XII, c. 26: *"Si fallor sum"*.

[101] *Matt.*, 6:27.

its behalf, reason, by itself, tells us nothing about the world. Aware of this, we are free to choose two courses. The first is to retreat into absolute or moderated scepticism. We can take the mental habits referred to above as our sole guide, and not worry about their lack of rational basis. We can carry on talking about morality, and sometimes even half believe ourselves—but only in so far as we wish to influence the behaviour of others who still believe the concept to have any clear meaning. Otherwise, we can accept that God exists, and that questions about His purpose in having placed us here are entirely proper. I should stress that I am not proving His existence in any general way. I am simply asserting its logical necessity for certain kinds of thinking. If we want to use the words 'right' and 'wrong' and 'rights' and 'nature', and want them to mean anything, we must understand that reason is not a self-contained entity, but a meditation on faith. It need on this account be no less powerful, nor usually any less deadly against credulous stupidy. It must nevertheless, be considered as a strictly secondary force. *Credo ut intellegam*, said Anselm—"I believe so that I may understand."[102]

V: Fundamentals of Christian Theism

Let us, then state what it is necessary for us to believe before we can hope to understand. In doing this, we also state the minimal assumptions of Christian theism:

First, there is a God, who is the supreme, benevolent Governor of the universe.

Second, He has established a code of morality, and dispenses punishments and rewards according to how we conform to it.

Whether or not either of these is true—or, if true, can be proven—is presently of no account. A Christian is defined by adherence to them. They underpin the thought of nearly everyone else. From the first, we deduce the existence of an orderly external world, and of ourselves within it through time. Being Supreme, God can be "the

---

[102] Anselm (1033-1109), *Proslogion*, cap. 1.

Maker and Preserver of all things, both visible and invisible".[103] Being benevolent, He is that Maker and Preserver. Otherwise, there must be a chance of my being a deluded spark of instantaneity, and everything else, including you, nothing at all. This would be incompatible with the Divine Nature as stated. From the second, we derive both an absolute morality and a firm reason for keeping to it.

VI: Natural Law and Morality

Furthermore, the existence of the world having been shown a necessary consequence of the first assumption, it seems reasonable to suppose that the various articles of this morality might be revealed to us, not merely by the directly inspired Word of God, but also by the fundamental nature of His Creation. We can seek guidance from Paul's Letter to the Romans—"Thou shalt not commit adultery, Thou shalt not kill, Thou shalt not steal, Thou shalt not bear false witness, Thou shalt not covet; and if there be any other commandment, it is briefly comprehended in this saying, namely, Thou shalt love thy neighbour as thyself."[104] Or, although our paths of reasoning merge only after having sprung from different sources, we are perhaps able now to agree with Aquinas that

> there is in man a first, innate inclination to good, which he shares with everything so far as it desires the maintenance of its existence according to its own nature. Through this, the natural law pertains to all that serves the continuation of human life and all that impedes death. Second, he is inclined to certain more specific ends according to the nature which he shares with the other animals. Those ends are termed part of the natural law 'which Nature has taught all animals'—such as the attraction of the sexes, and rearing of children, and like things. Third, he is inclined to good according to his rational nature, which nature is proper to man alone. So he is inclined by nature to seek knowledge of God, and to live in society. Under the

---

[103] From the First of the 39 Articles of Religion to which all Anglicans are supposed to assent.

[104] *Rom.*, 13:9.

heading of natural law come all acts pertaining to this inclination—chiefly that he should avoid ignorance, and be honest in his dealings, and all other such actions.[105]

VII: Reason and Revelation

These both might seem on first glance very different approaches to morality. But the first premise of our current scheme of arguing is that there is a fundamental harmony of reason and revelation. According to Aquinas, the specific nature of man is to use his mind, and to observe a morality which is rationally deducible by a process of observation. It is with regard to his reason that man is distinct as a species from the other animals. This is no necessary denial of those parts of his nature which are generic to him and all other things, in so far as these are required for his sustenance as a moral individual, or to the propagation of his species. According to Paul, we are obliged as God's creatures to a certain course of action. Some aspects of this he states explicitly. Others he leaves to our own finding, having indicated a method of finding them. It is evident that, if we are to follow this course, we must do whatever is conducive to following it most effectively. This surely means that, unless directed otherwise by our primary purpose as moral beings, we are to seek the continuation of our lives. Therefore, by whichever of the ways we care to proceed, there is no contradiction of the other. According to either, an act can be sinful in itself—directly against God or against nature—or, though apparently indifferent in itself, connected by association with whatever sin to which it might tend. To return to the example given above, my cutting of your throat for pleasure or gain would be a contravention both of Paul's injunction against killing, and of our natural requirement to be honest in our dealings with others. My merely producing the knife, on the other hand, would be indifferent or sinful depending on what use for the thing I had in mind.

---

[105] Thomas Aquinas (1226-74), *Summa Theologiæ*, I-II, 94, 2. The embedded quotation, *Quæ natura omnia animalia docuit*, is unidentified in my text. [I believe it is from Ulpian, a Roman lawyer of the 3d century – "which nature has taught every animal". SIG, January 2005]

All which having been said, we move to an examination of the first part of our question posed initially—namely, of those ways in which smoking might be held contrary to nature, or to the otherwise known will of God, and therefore in both cases sinful.

VIII: Smoking and Natural Law

Now, if there is any fact about smoking more certain than its dangers, it is that people find it enjoyable. Its very dangers, indeed, are testimony to its pleasures. Smoking kills, people are told; and they continue to smoke, even if in diminishing numbers. I recognise that I am discussing pleasures which I have never experienced, and which no person who has seems able to describe to me. But I am quite sure that they exist. Anyone who makes it his business to go about denying this is an unimaginative fool. Tobacco has many pleasant effects, and their type and degree is oddly contingent on what they are wanted to be. It can soothe the nerves after they have been strained. It can steady them when some particular act of judgment or resolve is called for. It makes the company of friends more cheerful. It makes up for lack of company. Smoking can be very enjoyable.

It is, moreover, the most universal of those pleasures which we do not also share with the animals. Just when and by what means the American Indians discovered to what use the cured leaf of the plant *nicotiana tabacum* could be put is unknown. But its use was the one Indian custom which the conquering Spaniards not only never tried suppressing, but actually themselves adopted. Once revealed to the world, it spread within a few decades to every part of humanity not absolutely shut away from foreign trade. Tobacco was smoked in England and in Spain, in Mecca and in Rome, in Russia, in China, in Japan. Peoples utterly dissimilar in every other respect of manners had tobacco smoking in common. No kind of religious observance, nor eating bread, nor drinking alcohol, were so widespread. Even in those times and places until recently where smoking was difficult or unfashionable, tobacco was instead chewed or ground up and sniffed. Use of the plant has been no passing craze. It is no custom, like eating hamburgers or wearing jeans, which has been associated with any particular way of life, and is often embraced or rejected as part of that greater whole. It is a pleasure common to the whole of mankind. No one who identifies pleasure with sin could ever fail to notice it. And that there have been, and still are, Christians who believe in this identity is undeniable.

IX: Pleasure and Sin: The Christian Case Against Puritanism

While there had been a small ascetic movement throughout the first three Christian centuries, it had its real beginning and most spectacular phase in the period following the conversion of the Roman Empire. Their faith no longer persecuted—and soon, indeed, became a condition for public advancement—the more severe Christians began withdrawing in great numbers into the Syrian and Egyptian deserts. They saw the pleasures and conveniences of city life as so many snares of the Devil. Their belief was that, the greater the misery they could suffer on earth, the more certain and the sweeter their bliss would be in Heaven. Their biographies stagger the mind. How much is recorded truth, and how much wishful thinking or plain falsehood, is often impossible to say. One Macarius of Alexandria is said to have slept in a marsh for six months, and to have welcomed the continual mosquito bites there as so many Divine gifts. Others of his kind are said to have carried iron weights strapped on their bodies, or to have passed whole months in clumps of thorn bushes, or to have fasted themselves into blindness, or to have eaten only filth, and that very seldom. They never washed or changed their clothes. Some crawled round under the Egyptian sun, naked except for their long hair. Of all these, though, none was so memorable as Simeon Stylites. A youth of thirteen when he left shepherding and became a monk, one of his penances was to tie a rope about himself so tight that parts of his body began putrefying. According to Antony, his devoted biographer, "[a] horrible stench, intolerable to the bystanders, exhaled from his body, and worms dropped from him wherever he stood, and they filled his bed."[106] At last, persuaded to leave his monastery, he ascended to the top of various columns, the last of which being sixty feet high and six wide. There he remained until his death, thirty years later. He is said once to have stood for an

---

[106] Quoted in William Edward Hartpole Lecky, *History of European Morals from Augustus to Charlemagne* (1869), Longmans, Green, London, 1911, vol. 2, p. 112.

entire year on one leg, the other covered by open ulcers. Antony perched beside him, picking up the maggots that fell down and replacing them. "Eat what God has given you", said Simeon.[107] He was among the most celebrated men of his age. Pilgrims visited him from as far away as India. The Emperor Theodosius II consulted him on affairs of state. His funeral procession was followed by the Patriarch of Antioch, a government minister, six bishops and a small army. His image is still to be seen, painted on church walls throughout the Eastern Patriarchates.

Our own history offers nothing quite so colourful as this. Thomas Beckett and Thomas More, our most famous ecclesiastics, both had ascetic turns of mind. But our closest national approximation was made by the Puritans of the seventeenth century. Some never closed their eyes without visions of hellfire crowding into their minds. Their loathing of everything frivolous, or even tending to enjoyment, amounted at times to a mania. "The Puritan hated bearbaiting" said Macaulay, "not because it gave pain to the bear, but because it gave pleasure to the spectators."[108] Their political ascendency no sooner began than was over. Their influence continued to be felt. It has certainly bequeathed us the most unendurable Sunday in the free world. Its afterglow may provide much of the energy to the anti-smoking pressure groups. Virginia Woolf's maternal grandfather was a pleasure-hating evangelical of the simplest kind. He smoked a cigar once, "and found it so delicious that he never smoked again."[109] This is perhaps to be expected. But the same views were held by many Victorians who had abandoned every other tenet of their childhood faith. Frances Newman, younger brother of Cardinal John Henry Newman, though an ardent free thinker and radical, was just as strongly against tobacco—and, for that matter, alcohol, bright clothes and sex.

---

[107] *Ibid.*

[108] Macaulay *History, op. cit.*, vol. 1, p. 129 (or, in other editions, the eleventh paragraph of chapter II).

[109] Leslie Stephen (the novelist's father), quoted in Gertrude Himmelfarb, *Victorian Minds*, Weidenfield & Nicolson, London, 1968, p. 310.

When I was first at school, I came across a boy who seemed as capable as anyone else of observing the world, but who had drawn a very strange conclusion. He had noticed how, when he fell and cut himself, our teacher would rush over and comfort him with plasters and little hugs. Sometimes, she would even let him off punishments for what he had done earlier in the day. Therefore, whenever he felt neglected, or thought he had done anything slightly naughty, he would stab some part of his body with a compass until he began to bleed. Fifteen hundred years ago, he would have grown into a desert saint. Alive today in the Philippines, he would long since have taken to pushing skewers through his cheeks, or cutting his nipples off. As it is, he may well currently be a noted puritan in his own little circle. There would be no change of attitude required. The association of pain with holiness is one less of logic than of psychology. To hope that those martyred in His Name earn some special favour in the eyes of God is perfectly reasonable. It is, at any rate, a credit to humanity. To suppose that anyone can gain grace simply by rotting away, of his own volition, on top of a column, or denying himself every bodily pleasure, is childishly absurd. In so far as the ascetic state hinders the rational function of mankind—and its more extreme varieties certainly must[110]—it is against nature. Even the purely negative varieties are an abuse of it. Anyone who has laughed for five minutes at a time, or chatted awhile with friends, will know how generally good some kinds of enjoyment are to the body and soul. There are texts in the Bible which, taken in isolation, approve the self-denial of

---

[110] See Gibbon:

> This voluntary martyrdom [of Simeon Stylites] must have gradually destroyed the sensibility both of the mind and body; nor can it be presumed that the fanatics who torment themselves are susceptible of any lively affection for the rest of mankind. A cruel, unfeeling temper has distinguished the monks of every age and country: their stern indifference, which is seldom mollified by personal friendship, is inflamed by religious hatred; and their merciless zeal has strenuously administered the holy office of the Inquisition (Gibbon, *op. cit.*, vol. 4 [chapter XXXVII], p. 18).

every pleasure.[111] But a fine answer to anyone who delights in finding these and bringing them out when others look happy, is to read from that entire book which opens with the words "[l]et him kiss me with the kisses of his mouth: for thy love is better than wine";[112] and continue till he goes away or faints with shock. Christ himself appreciated the pleasures of friendship. Certain theologians can put whatever bizarre gloss on it which takes their fancy. To any candid reader, the Last Supper can only be a touchingly human occasion. Here is a man facing inevitable death. Does he pass his last evening in a final round of fanatic penances? He does nothing of the sort. He arranges a dinner with his friends. "With desire I have desired to eat this passover with you before I suffer" he tells them.[113] He tries letting them down gently from their expectations of what his kingdom will consist in. Exactly what he would have made of Simeon Stylites is rather hard to imagine. Very likely, he would not have approved. Almost certainly, he would not have been approved of.

Pleasure cannot be regarded as bad. In many respects, it is as proper to our nature as is eating or sleeping. But, of course, this is no end to the matter. Though pleasure is not in itself bad, only certain kinds of it can be thought entirely legitimate; and there are many kinds which are absolutely illegitimate. That kind potentially involved in murder has already been discussed. It remains open to say that smoking comes into the class of illegitimate pleasures.

---

[111] See, for a very notorious instance of this, Eusebius, *History of the Church*, Book V, c. 8. When about twenty years old, Origen of Alexandria, an enthusiast from his earliest boyhood, considered the text of Matthew, 19:12—"For there are some eunuchs, which were so born from their mother's womb: and there are some eunuchs which were made eunuchs of men: and there be eunuchs which have made themselves eunuchs for the kingdom of heaven's sake. He that is able to receive it, let him receive it." His mind made up, he immediately castrated himself. He realised only some while later that his exegesis had been too literal. His story can be taken as illustrating more than one moral.

[112] *Song of Solomon*, 1:2.

[113] *Luke*, 22:15.

X: The Issue of "Addiction"

It can, in the first place, be called an addiction—this is to say, a subordination of the rational faculty to the purely animal appetites. If indeed this, it could be likened to alcoholism; and "[b]e not among winebibbers" says Solomon; for he shall come to poverty.[114] Nor, says Paul, shall he inherit the Kingdom of Heaven.[115] Efforts to prove that smoking really is a similar activity form a considerable share of the medical and polemical literature on the subject. I return to M. A. H. Russell, already quoted above. "Cigarette smoking" he says, "is probably the most addictive and dependence-producing object-specific self-administered gratification known to man."[116] He continues elsewhere that "[n]ot with alcohol, cannabis and possibly even heroin is the addiction so easily acquired."[117] "[I]t requires no more than three or four casual cigarettes during adolescence virtually to ensure that a person will become a regular dependent smoker."[118] 'Once a smoker—always a smoker.' This is only a slight exaggeration. It is unlikely that more than one in four smokers succeeds in giving it up for good before the age of sixty.[119] Certainly, if the regular smoker could be identified with the habitual drunkard or opiate addict, the natural law verdict would be a foregone conclusion. But it is open at least to doubt whether this has been properly done. If we follow the usual medical definition, drug addiction, or—to adopt the favoured terminology of the World Health Organisation since 1964—drug dependence, requires for its diagnosis the joint presence of three conditions. First, there is the pleasurable alteration of mood. Second,

---

[114] *Prov.*, 23:20-21.

[115] I *Cor.*, 6:10.

[116] M.A.H. Russell in 1976, quoted in Ashton & Stepney, *op. cit.*, p. 53.

[117] M.A.H. Russell in 1977, quoted in *ibid.*, p. 140.

[118] M.A.H. Russell in 1971, quoted in *ibid.*

[119] M.A.H. Russell in 1977, quoted in *ibid.*

there is an increasing tolerance of whatever substance is taken, with a concomitantly required increase of dose to maintain its effect. Third, there is the occurrence of pain, mental or physical, on the ending of regular indulgence. Let us see to what extent these are characteristic of cigarette smoking.

Its pleasurable effects I have already mentioned. These are real enough. The plain fact, however, is that they differ from what we normally call intoxication not merely in degree, but also in nature. The effect of alcohol is to dull or even to suspend the workings of our more rational nature. Continued indulgence, on a large enough scale, is enough entirely to destroy them. The effect of nicotine is simply to alter them in various, comparatively mild, ways. No person of reasonably firm mind will go out of his way to avoid a group of people in the street just because he suspects most of them to have been smoking. Nor, if he is driving, will he feel inclined to slow down or move into another lane if he notices in front of him another driver who, to his certain knowledge, has smoked five cigarettes earlier in the evening. No one—at least, to my present knowledge—has ever smoked himself into an ungovernable rage, nor, for that matter, into Cardboard City. Assuming decent ventilation, I have never once thought any conversation with smokers a waste of my time simply on account of their smoking. It cannot, therefore, be said that the pleasures of the activity are in themselves gross and animalistic.

The broad pattern of alcoholism is too well-known to require much telling. It begins usually with the drinking in company of ale and beer or the lighter wines. These soon having lost their satisfying effect, it then progresses, either directly or through the fortified wines, to spirits. The point is eventually reached where, to produce the desired effect, amounts of alcohol are regularly consumed which would kill a moderate drinker or teetotaller several times over. This pattern is common to many other drugs. Dependence on amphetamine has been known to lead to a progressive escalation of dose from a daily 10mg to 1,000mg. The same is often true of heroin and the other opiates. It is not the case with nicotine. Many smokers do move on from an initial five or ten cigarettes per day to twenty or even forty, but hardly ever go beyond this. True, there are practical limits on the number of cigarettes that can be smoked per day: even one every fifteen minutes only amounts to sixty in fifteen hours. But it would be possible to increase the amount of nicotine absorbed by inhaling more deeply, or changing to stronger cigarettes or to cigars or to using a pipe. There is no evidence that this happens to any considerable extent. The evidence seems, indeed, to indicate that there is no need for much escalation of dose. After even years of regular smoking, those areas of the brain affected by nicotine retain most of their initial sensitivity.[120] No hardened spirit drinker will regard a pint of weak lager first thing in the morning as anything but distinctly second best—and perhaps not even as that. A smoker tends to find one favourite brand of cigarette and thereafter to stay loyal to it; and each morning's first lighting up, in the absence of any breakdown of health, remains no less pleasurable.

Some smokers do come to rely on their cigarettes to an extent where giving them up is an often painful effort. Yet giving up typically involves a depression and irritability which becomes fairly intense after a day or so, and then steadily reduces. But there is nothing about the initial physiological effects comparable with the hallucinations and convulsions that the normal alcoholic feels on drying out. It seems, also, that only a minority of smokers are dependent on nicotine. According to Russell himself, this becomes apparent only when twenty or more cigarettes are smoked per day.[121] Yet, in a survey of British smoking habits the results of which were published in 1980, 25 per cent of current smokers claimed a daily consumption of ten cigarettes or less; and 62 per cent of female and 48 per cent of male smokers claimed one of twenty or less.[122] It should also be said that, in the ten years to 1987, 20 per cent of British smokers are believed to have given up.[123] These figures hardly support Russell's

---

[120] For a fuller discussion of this point (of which my own is very largely an abridgement), see Ashton & Stepney, *op. cit.*, pp. 58-60.

[121] M.A.H. Russell in 1980, quoted in Ashton & Stepney, *op. cit.*, p. 141.

[122] Office of Population Censuses and Surveys, 1980, quoted *ibid.*

[123] Whitaker, *op. cit.*, p. 153.

bolder assertions. Even with heavier smokers, there are too many instances of a sudden stopping without apparent withdrawal symptoms for the normal concept of dependence to apply in full.

XI: Is Smoking "Unnatural"?

In the second place, in the argument over its legitimacy as a pleasure, smoking might be said to involve an unnatural use of a bodily function. "If God had wanted us to smoke" the saying goes, "he would have given us chimneys out of our heads". Plainly, it requires the drawing of tobacco smoke into the lungs, where nicotine can be absorbed into the bloodstream and carried thence to the brain.

Equally plainly, the lungs are not suited to this function; and they quite often fail under the strain put on them. But, to the extent that the natural function of the lungs is to introduce oxygen into the lungs, and that natural functions represent the will of God, it does not automatically follow that smoking is sinful. There was a time when it was believed that it had a useful medical purpose. It was thought a good prophylactic against the plague, and a cure for, among other maladies, headaches, gout and scabies. As late as 1901, the pharmacological authority, W. Hale-White, actually recommended it for the treatment of respiratory disorders.[124] So long as this belief could be held, smoking, whatever its general merits, could be regarded as a proper activity within certain limits—just as puncturing the veins with needles is not today thought improper when its purpose is the maintenance or restoration of health. The present medical consensus is that tobacco has no therapeutic value. This consensus can, however, be challenged. One of the main purposes of the anti-smoking lobby, it seems is to link smoking with as many illnesses and defects of character as is humanly possible.

Thus, it has by now been associated with everything from child beating to sleeplessness, and from careless driving to ulcers. Unlike with the various cancers, however, the precise causal sequence in these cases has not been fully established. It is possible that people who smoke increase their chances thereby of suffering these things.

---

[124] Whitaker, *op. cit.*, p. 146.

It might, on the other hand, be that those people already likely to suffer them are drawn to smoking; and that smoking might—admittedly at the possible cost of more serious problems later—alleviate them. In its essentials, this is no new argument. The late T. E. Utley was convinced that tobacco, with its soothing effects, had prevented many suicides and the occasional murder.[125] Writing some years ago in *The Guardian*, Polly Toynbee declared that "I don't want to scream and yell at the family, so I smoke."[126] Around the same time, in the *The Daily Telegraph*, David Loshak put the same more general case as stated above.[127] Granting it were a correct one, smoking would not be an unnatural activity for such people. As Aquinas said, when discussing the concept of "nature", it may be "that something which is against human nature, as it may pertain either to reason or to the health of the body, may become natural to a man because of a certain deficiency in his nature."[128]

XII: Is Smoking "Slow Suicide"?

Even if it definitely were shown not necessary in some people for the preservation of their health—or necessary in only an inconsiderable minority—it still would not have to follow that smoking were sinful. Going to Aquinas again, he doubts that uses of limbs or organs contrary to their apparent functions are in themselves bad. It need not be true 'that he sins who, for example, walks on his hands, or does with his feet anything which is more appropriately done with his hands.'[129] Such acts become sinful only to the extent that they might

---

[125] See his article, "Lighting up for Liberty", in *The Times*, London, 3rd August 1987.

[126] See her article of that title in *The Guardian*, London and Manchester, 25th May 1981.

[127] David Loshak, "A whiff of consolation for the smoker", *The Daily Telegraph*, London, 30th October 1981.

[128] Thomas Aquinas, *Summa Theologiæ*, I-II, 30, 4.

[129] Thomas Aquinas, *Summa Contra Gentiles*, Lib. III, cap. cxxii. His main topic of discussion here is the interesting, and perhaps important, issue of whether

impede a man's nature. Obviously, the tendency of smoking is to shorten life, and this is about as severe an impediment as can be imagined. But not every shortening of life is equally a sin, or even actually sinful. As an act, it falls into not one but several categories. Before we can decide the status of smoking, we must first investigate into which of these its life-shortening tendency falls.

In 1658, the Jesuit priest, Jakob Baldé, asked in a tract published in Nuremberg against smoking "[w]hat difference is there between a smoker and a suicide; except that the one takes longer to kill himself than the other?"[130] Medicine being then in its infancy, and there being a complete lack of any statistical evidence for his claim, Baldé should not be seen as some remote precursor of the Royal College of Physicians. He wrote at a time when smoking tobacco was a comparatively new activity in Europe, and, as said above, was illegal in many parts of it. What we have in this instance is, as part of a wider denunciation, a rhetorical flourish decked out with supporting evidence drawn from anecdote. Removed, however, from its particular historical context, this is an extremely grave allegation, and one which, if ever made out, would be final condemnation of smoking in Christian terms. For suicide is unequivocally a sin. It is a crime against human nature as defined above. It is held strictly analogous to murder—the separation by man of a union of body and soul made by God.[131] It has, indeed, often been thought worse than murder—as a cowardly flight from those apparent sufferings by which God, in His infinite mercy, tests and refines His creatures.[132] Three and a third centuries after Baldé, the harmful effects of tobacco have been made out with an often alarming weight of evidence. It might be thought that the modern posters which I have

---

fornication and sodomy involve an unnatural emission of sperm, and so hinder procreation.

[130] Quoted, Ashton & Stepney, *op. cit.*, p. 4.

[131] On this point, see Augustine, *op. cit.*, Lib. I, cap. 19.

[132] For a most inspiring example of Divine benevolence in this respect, see the *Book of Job*.

seen put up in hospitals—telling me that "Smoking is slow Suicide"—had unquestionable authority behind them. They have not. That smoking tends to shorten life is undeniable. But, no less undeniably, the mere shortening of life is not always suicide. If it were, the conventional judgments in church history would be radically at fault.

The anti-Catholic laws of the sixteenth and seventeenth centuries are one of the very few reasons for an Englishman to be ashamed of his history. Justifications have been attempted. But every persecution has been claimed by someone as necessary; and the merits of this one are no more nor less than any other. Lay adherents of the old religion were heavily discriminated against by law. Any of their priests arrested on English soil were subject, on proof of their status, to being hanged, then cut down while still alive, and disembowelled, castrated and dismembered. It was a horrible death; and it was made more horrible still when inflicted in the presence of a mob screaming its delight, and attended by every means of ensuring that the victim remained conscious as long as possible. Despite this, the English Mission was never short of recruits. Priests continued volunteering to come into England and perform those rites believed necessary for the salvation of those who remained Catholics here. One such was Thomas Macclesfield. He was arrested almost as soon as he landed. He was promised his release if only he would take the Oath of Allegiance to James I, so acknowledging his ecclesiastical jurisdiction under the Act of Supremacy. This was a real offer. It had been made to George Napper, another priest, in 1589. He had taken the Oath, and had been released. Another priest, Ralph Sherwin, though he turned it down, had even been offered an bishopric if he would only save his life. Macclesfield refused all inducements. The Pope was head of Christendom without rival or colleague, he asserted. He was hanged, drawn and quartered on the 1st July, 1616. He was aged 26. The youngest victim of this persecution that I can find was a youth of nineteen called James Bird. He refused the Oath, and was butchered in 1593. They died for their refusal to repeat a few dozen words which millions of others had repeated without hesitation, and which hundreds of thousands had repeated without believing. They died for what many, then and since, would call a trifle. To call their deaths suicide, however, would show not merely a gross lack of principle, but also a defective imagination. The Roman Church has canonised or beatified each of them.

Towards the end of the sixth century, there was a Bishop Salvius of Albi in France. During that century, the Mediterranean world had been swept by a wave of the most tremendous epidemics. At Constantinople, on the first appearance of the plague, in the year 542, the historian Procopius records that ten thousand people a day had died throughout the four summer months.[133] All order had for a while collapsed, as the normal bonds of one person to another were severed by fear. The sick were left to die untended. The healthy threw themselves into a round of orgies and rioting. Even outside the towns, whole regions became deserted, so that the crops rotted in the fields, and the cows went unmilked. At the first sign of plague in Albi, the usual panic occurred. People fled, leaving the sick behind. Salvius stayed with them. Whether by ordinary nursing or miracle, he kept the death rate below the level of catastrophe; and the epidemic abated. But he was one of its last victims.

His example is one chosen at random. There have been countless others, before and since. I think of the Belgian missionary, Joseph de Veuster, sent at his own request in 1873 to a leper colony in the Hawaiian Islands. He caught the disease himself, and died, still tending the sick, in 1889. A man who runs into a burning house to save a child is rightly thought brave. There are not words to describe someone who voluntarily and with premeditation risks life or health in the service of the infectious sick. Salvius was canonised. De Veuster is now called 'Venerable'.

But not every life-shortening act has been approved. There was in Africa once an heretical sect known as the Donatist Circumcelliones. Its members had conceived such a hatred of life and desire for martyrdom, that, driven by joyous frenzies, they would sometimes leap in great numbers from high cliffs, so that the rocks below were

---

[133] Procopius, *De Bello Persico*, Lib. XXIII, cap. 1. See also J. N. Biraben and J. le Goff, "La Peste dans le Haut Moyen Age", in *Annales: Economies, Sociétés, Civilisations*, 24 (1969), pp. 1484-1510.

splashed red with their blood. Sometimes, they would stop travellers on the roads, and oblige them to inflict a killing blow, by the promise of a reward if they consented, and the threat of murder if they refused. This was accounted suicide.

There was another sect of heretics, this one in France, called the Albigenses. Many of these also wanted martyrdom. Their methods of seeking it—at least, before the Papacy took action against them—was rather more subtle. If ill, they would accelerate or provoke death, by fasting and occasionally by bleeding. These practices were accounted suicide.

The clear distinguishing principle in these instances is primary intention. In the first two, death was an effect of voluntary action. It was, however, a secondary consequence, a byproduct of something done with an entirely different main end in view. The recusants probably had no great wish to go through an agonising death. But, faced with this or apostasy from what they believed was absolutely true and right, they resolutely chose the lesser of evils. No more can it be thought that Salvius and De Veuster were seeking death directly. In the second two instances, it was sought directly—not, perhaps, as an end in itself, as the self-overdosing of some jilted shorthand typist of our own day might be presumed; but it was still sought for no predominating earthly reason. If I put a gun to my head, or lie in a hot bath and open a vein, my primary intention, in all probability, is self-destruction. If I light a cigarette, it is to absorb nicotine into my body. The one act is to end life. The other, in my own estimation, is to enhance it. If one effect of the second is to bring my death forward in some unknowable degree, this is not suicide. If I could somehow know that, by lighting up, I should be 'spending' a given number of minutes, it would still not be suicide. If I had it on the highest medical authority that one cigarette would kill me after five minutes, it would, again, still not be suicide. The same distinguishing principle applies as above. There may be no comparison between my own seeking of pleasure at inordinate cost, and the laying down by someone else of his life for the sake of others or in praising or holding fast to his God. But the sin involved here would be that of addiction—most definitely not of suicide. But this is an unlikely situation. In normal circumstances, the seeking of pleasure will be at an uncertain and perhaps long-delayed price.

In truth, the best analogy of smoking is not suicide, but working at a dangerous occupation. Take coal miners, for example. They notoriously place themselves in danger. Working at the coal face, they risk burial alive by collapsing tunnels; they risk being burned to death or suffocated by poisonous gasses. Even without these exceptional events, the environment of a coal mine is unhealthy. The air is loaded with silicious dust. Breathing it often leads to pneumoconiosis, a fatal lung disease. Crawling about for long periods places unnatural strain on the knee joints, causing arthritis. The wages offered for coal mining reflect these dangers. The work is for the most part unskilled manual labour. It requires endurance and some strength, but little in the way of initiative. In as much, then, as the wages offered are higher than those paid for labour of the same general grade on the surface, they incorporate a special premium for risk. They are an incentive for a man to put his life or long-term health in danger.

Now, whatever may be the state of affairs in other parts of the world, in this country, no one is compelled to take up any specific occupation. If a man decides to accept a coal miner's wages, rather than those of a shelf-stacker or static security guard, or of whatever other menial occupation might be open to him, he does so of his own volition. Perhaps his father and elder brothers were miners before him. Leaving aside any sentimental talk of tradition, the real meaning of this is that he will have had an excellent chance of learning the dangers of the job. Perhaps he is married with children. If so, he might have done well considering how he was to fill these extra mouths before bringing them into the world. And even the worst paid job nowadays keeps a family from starving; and the Department of Social Security is often amazingly generous with the taxpayers' money. Anyone who goes down a coal mine does so either because he is stupid, or because he prefers the present satisfactions that the extra money can buy to his continued health in the future. If he goes down for the money, the only difference between him and a smoker is that the smoker combines his pleasure and danger in a single act; and he keeps them distinct. I have listened to much invective against the miners. But I have never heard them called sinners by mere virtue of their occupation. Yet, if to smoke be a sin on the grounds of its unnaturalness, so equally must digging coal be one.

XIII: Smoking, Sin and Toleration

This is my answer to the first part of our main question, then—that smoking, in whatever light we care to regard it, is just not sinful. Even, however, if it were—even if it were shown as plainly against Scripture and nature as throat cutting, and the smoker unquestionably doomed to the lake of black fire—my answer to the second part of that main question would remain unaltered. Ambrose and many of the Church Fathers, together with theologians of nearly every Christian sect since, have asserted that to tolerate sin is to partake of sin. That this is not so, however, is as necessary a consequence of our two minimal assumptions given above as those by which we prove our own existence. To see this, we return to those assumptions; and, from them, we derive two further secondary principles.

The first of these is that the human will is free. Now, there is no reason in itself to doubt that every event is predetermined, and every soul marked out from the beginning of time for salvation or damnation. But, most plainly, it contradicts our first assumption, of a benevolent God. To see this, suppose I were to train a child of mine to love starting fires, to love the act of kindling flame more than anything else in the world. Suppose then I were to hand him a box of matches and lock him into a fuel store. I could, perhaps, blame what remained of him for the ensuing explosion—just as God could damn a murderer, having been knowingly the first cause of the murder, and the murderer himself just the final link in the chain of causation. My determining influence on the child's actions must be infinitely smaller than that of God on the murderer, yet who would call me a just or loving father, except from fear of offending me? To generalise from this, careless mistakes aside, there is no action whatever we can call sinful where there is no voluntary participation. We laugh at Xerxes, who had the Hellespont scourged for washing his bridge away. Are we to say God is equally childish and arbitrary?

Certainly, taking the will as free brings its own problems. It may save the notion of Divine Benevolence, but only, it seems, by compromising that omniscience which is implicit in the notion of Divine Supremacy. Either God knew, long before He created the universe, that a certain murder would take place, or He did not. If He did know, then all our talk of free will is so much more *flatus uocis*. As with the child and matches, when I see that something will happen, there is always an element of contingency about its happening. When God, in His omniscience, foresees an event, it becomes inevitable. To say otherwise is to state a contradiction. According to Boethius, this is not a real problem. In his view, God is an atemporal being. We exist in time, and are aware of a past and future. God is outside of this continuum; and He therefore can have no foreknowledge, everything occurring in an immediate, eternal present.[134] This is an ingenious solution, and it may possibly be the real one. But, however we choose to justify it, that the will is free we must believe, or we must abandon the concept of God given above. It is a necessary assumption, following on from our first.

The second question we have already touched, in our discussion of suicide. It concerns what facts God takes into account when delivering His Judgment on each soul—actions or intentions? Our own earthly law, though it sometimes tries its best to do otherwise, can, by and large, judge only according to actions, all else being too uncertain to sway the verdict. To the Divine Court, though, nothing is uncertain. If I were to throw coins at a beggar, hoping without success to break his head, the law of the land would have to regard my action as charitable, if suspect. But, to God, my intent to commit murder—even my precise degree of resolve in the matter—would be perfectly clear, and so a cognisable fact in reaching His Verdict. 'If we have forgotten the Name of our God, and holden up our hands to any strange God: shall not God search it out? For he knoweth the very secrets of the heart.'[135] Hence, we can sin against Divine Law both with our bodies and in our hearts.

Yet, this being said, it seems unreasonable to claim all breaches of

---

[134] Boethius, *De Consolatione Philosophiæ*, Lib. V, cap. 90-105.

[135] *Ps.*, 44:21.

that law as being equally serious—a desire to commit genocide, an actual rape, an evil intention bungled and producing only good: all equal grounds for damnation. Go back again to the example of my cutting your throat: if I no more than contemplate the action, I harm only my own prospects of salvation. If I make my intention actual, I also harm another soul, which I may have prevented from excelling in a life of subsequent virtue. To intend is clearly easier than to act; yet, to know myself damned already for the former, what more have I to lose by effecting the latter? The notion is plainly unreasonable, since, so far from deterring, after a very low point, it even encourages sin. Granted, anything is conceivable of God, and there may well be some divine equivalent of the English conspiracy laws. But to suppose this is again an evident contradiction of our first assumption. It seems better to accord putting our sins into an order of gravity, or adopting the Roman division of them into venial and mortal. Or we might instead conceive each to carry a given number of points, a sufficient number earned resulting in one's damnation. There can be no certainty on details here, but there can be little dispute whether actual sins are not judged more severely than potential ones.

So we take it that man is a creature capable of freely choosing good or evil, and is judged on how he chooses. Now, in the wild, isolated from others, our opportunities for choosing either are at best limited. Without others round us, our actions must be morally neutral for the most part, only those affecting ourselves and God counting—among these being suicide, masturbation, blasphemy, and the like. Even those sins we could commit in our hearts would be limited by our ignorance of what sins there were to commit. However, it being part of our nature to live in society, this problem seldom faces us. Living in close proximity to others, we find fresh opportunities with each new day for shining in God's eyes, or not. And, in so far as our contact with others increases, so increase our opportunities; and, in so far as it is diminished, so our opportunities are diminished. Which brings us to the logical outcome of our two assumptions. God's full sanction is reserved for those societies alone of which the members can in the greatest degree possible choose good or evil for themselves: any other is a frustration of His Plan.

This outcome stated, we are able to go on and, in descending order of abstraction, derive its practical consequences. We first consider the proper role of government. Now, it does, by its very nature, involve coercion. It exists only by levying taxes, which are had from those who might well have used the money otherwise, to secure grace or damnation. It acts only by interfering with what people do, compelling some things, forbidding others. It is inevitably a hindrance to the free choice of good or evil by its subjects. But, while evidently God abhors the regulating of human action for its own sake, equally He cannot approve the possession of more freedom than is compatible with its own survival. Without some government—perhaps only protecting life and property—such chaos might result that either society would dissolve, or it would fall into the hands of some tyrant, who might promise stability, but deliver somewhat more. If this were so, there would be a Christian case for government. And since both the common sense of mankind and the overwhelming balance of the philosophers believe it so, reasoning as theologians, we may provisionally accept that government must exist. Moreover, letting it keep the internal peace, only a fool would deny it the means of foreign defence. Of course, the mode and degree appropriate to each nation differs, and no one kind is suitable to all. But it must be said that spending on armaments may never without sin be greater than is needed for bare defence against aggression. England needs a great navy, and in the modern world, a great air force. Unhappily, we must also have a nuclear deterrent of sorts. But whether we need an army of occupation or defence constantly in Germany seems quite another matter—as is whether we need bases in Cyprus and Hong Kong. In deciding, we must think as strategists and not as theologians; though we require no great depth of learning to see from our own past that having so many distant commitments is to cast a net for troubles.

We come now to the matter of personal conduct, with particular reference to smoking. It ought to be clear from what has already been said that the Christian should stand for the absolute realisable maximum of individual freedom. The only justification of State interference, apart from the protection of others, is the avoidance of collapse into chaos or tyranny. Whether or not smoking might be a threat to others is, as I said at the beginning, a matter which falls outside the scope of this present study. But, as it affects the soul of the smoker, there is no case for control. To be sure, increasing taxes on tobacco products would, in at least some measure, diminish consumption of them. Restricting advertising, it is sometimes argued, might have the same effect. Such measures might well cause many of those inclined to smoking either to think again, or not be reminded so forcibly or often of their inclination. Desiring to sin—always, of course, assuming the sinfulness of smoking—yet not actively sinning, they might avoid some of the pain decreed by God as their punishment. But holding people from evil holds them also from good. No longer are they allowed to confront their sinful longings for cigarettes, to fight them, and overcome them by act of will and piety alone, so gaining salvation. Directed with skill and effort, the law might vastly diminish smoking; but the resulting virtue would like that of a chaste eunuch—derived not from conquest of temptation, but from its absence. Without any overriding excuse of the public order, for any government to try encouraging or prohibiting various kinds of private conduct, is to frustrate the whole purpose of society—which is to be the stage on which we act under the watchful eye of God.[136]

XIV: The Evil of Moral Authoritarianism

Moral authoritarianism is far worse than any amount of tobacco product advertising. The authoritarian will be held responsible for

---

[136] See Aquinas:

> Human law does not prohibit every vice from which virtuous men abstain, but only the graver vices ... [which] ... unless prohibited would make it impossible for human society to endure (*Summa Theologiæ*, I-II, 96, 2).

In isolation, this might be taken as stark dissent from the position of Ambrose. In many ways, indeed, Aquinas deserves a high place in the history of libertarian thought. But, in spite of this, he was also a Catholic theologian of the thirteenth century; and, though he stood firmly against that insane bigotry which tears societies apart, he did not oppose intolerance in itself. On this point, see *ibid.*, II-II, 8 & 10.

the damnation of any souls on account of his having denied their right to choose good of their own accord, desire to sin overcome. The advertiser and his accomplices will find the path to Heaven much smoother. By offering temptation, they provoke choice. Therefore, they may cause the salvation of many who would otherwise have let themselves fall into Hell for lack of positive virtue.

Considered only in themselves, restrictions on smoking are bad. In this country, they are bad also on account of the means by which they have largely been imposed. Most people, if asked what it is that distinguishes a free society from tyranny, will perhaps think first of democracy. As modes of government go, this is a very fine one. But it is not the fundamental point of difference. Freedom relies above all else on the concept of what some call bourgeois legality and others the rule of law. Everyone who is not completely besotted by its power, knows that the State is a frighteningly dangerous institution. It may be a very necessary one. Tolerating its existence may be the only means available to us of seeing off or keeping at bay those other smaller dangers which threaten us. But it is useful only so far as it is kept within close restraints. In all dealings with its subjects, it must be forced to act in strict accordance with certain general rules of conduct, clearly stated in advance. These must apply equally to all citizens. Any dispute on either side as to their meaning must be resolved before independent and impartial courts of law. Where restrictions on smoking are concerned, this principle has been repeatedly flouted.

Twenty years ago, the Wilson Government decided that something had to be done about smoking. The first undeniable correlations with disease were being announced; and a government which interfered in everything else saw no principled objection to interfering with the tobacco industry. But it had no time for making laws. In the first place, the Parliamentary timetable was already full to overflowing. Making laws on one thing meant not making laws on something else. In the second, there was no consensus of opinion, either in the country as a whole, or, at that time, in the Labour Party, for anti-smoking legislation not to be time-wastingly controversial. And so, it resorted to threats. Kenneth Robinson, the Minister of Health, proudly recalls how he called the representatives of the leading companies to discussions with him, and bullied them into a "voluntary agreement". "There was always a slight hint that the government would legislate" he says, "a hint of blackmail in the background. I used it progressively as the talks went on and on. I used to throw up my hands and say, 'Gentlemen, if you can't agree, you leave me no alternative'."[137] From then until now, this has been the chosen method of restricting the promotion of tobacco products.

To say "Do as I tell you, or I will consider making a law to compel you" is the same as saying "Do as I tell you". In constitutional theory, no State official in this country has any more authority than is prescribed by law; and disputes over the use of that authority are referable if not to the normal courts of law, then certainly to various administrative tribunals which usually follow a legalistic procedure. Ministerial "blackmail" is a perfect means of escaping these burdensome restraints. On paper, they remain as formidable as ever they were. In reality, the principles of judicial review become as vital to the governing of this country as the principles of heraldry. The way is opened to omnipotent government, and the destruction of freedom.

Before moving on to a general conclusion, there are two clarifications needed, for the avoidance of misunderstanding.

First, to say that people should be left to go to Heaven or Hell by whatever means they see fit is not to show any lack of concern for them. Just as no libertarian wishes to see them smoking themselves into illness or an early grave, so no Christian can fail to worry about what may lie in wait for them beyond the grave. That in neither instance is coercion the required answer is no reason to stop caring. In both, the degree of caring is limited only by the requirement that we respect the autonomy of others, and by the normal rules of good taste. To see this, imagine that I, believing in the dangers—whatever these might be—of smoking, were confronted by a smoker. No one likes being pestered by proselytising strangers, as anyone who has

---

[137] Narrated Peter Taylor, in *Smoke Ring: The Politics of Tobacco*, The Bodley Head, London, 1984, p. 83.

been stopped in Central London by Moonies or Iranian refugees will readily admit. The chances of someone's being more than annoyed by such an intrusion are so generally low that it would hardly be worth the effort of beginning a lecture on the evils of tobacco. A total stranger, then, I would leave alone, other than, perhaps, to ask him to put his cigarette out if we were in an enclosed space, or whether he minded my opening a window to disperse the smoke. Someone I knew rather better I might, with sniffs and sour looks, let know what I felt. With a closer friend I might feel rather bolder. With a very close friend or relation—especially one actually suffering from what I had reason to believe an illness caused or worsened by smoking—there would be no restraint. I might beg him to put the cigarette out. I might try shaming him to put it out. I might force on his attention the various costs of smoking. I would do everything short of snatching the cigarette out of his mouth and putting it out myself. There is no contradiction between concern for others and respect for them, so long as each feeling is kept within its proper bounds.

Second, just because a law is unnecessary or harmful, is not normally sufficient reason for ostentatiously breaking it—nor for trying to bring down whatever government may have imposed it. Every government in history has made or enforced some laws which might be said to have failed the test set for them above. Our own statute book is already blemished. Effective measures to curb smoking would be a scandalous blemish on it. They would be arguably superfluous to the protection of others. In theological terms, they would be evil. Nor, believing them improper beyond all common doubt, would there be any strict obligation to obey such commands. We should be free in conscience to ignore them as suited our private pleasure.[138] But to say aloud to everyone that a bad law may rightly be

---

[138] This is no revolutionary assertion of rights. Without going through the constitutional documents of British and American history, I turn again to Aquinas:

> Laws may for two reasons be unjust. First, they may be contrary to the good of mankind ... either with regard to their end—as when a ruler imposes laws which are burdensome and designed not for the common good, but his own rapacity or vanity—or with regard to their maker—if,

broken is something else entirely. To make a cult of civil disobedience—as a whole section of our political class appears to have done—is often only slightly less than preaching rebellion. It opens the way to a contempt of law in general, and by those least able to tell what is bad from what merely inconvenient. This is not to condemn all resistance—certainly not in cases of open tyranny. But, recalling what its effects most usually are, it remains that, whatever their deeds or policy, active resistance to the authorities should normally be a last resort. This is obviously true in England, where, despite a century of increasing misgovernment, we can still call our laws and institutions on the whole sound, and can still agree to accept specific imperfections pending their reform. It applies with equal force, however, in the case of foreign countries. For, on the principle stated and explained above, in this less than perfect world to claim the Divine Sanction, a society need only enjoy the greatest degree of freedom possible, whatever more of it could be thought desirable. And so, to any reasonable man who may consider the overthrow of a bad government, the proper question is not—as the modern intellectual might occasionally pause to ask—whether he really will be assaulting something unspeakably evil, but to what extent his acting can result in any better state of affairs.[139]

XV: Conclusions

This, then, is what can be said about smoking. It is not an addiction

---

for example, he should go beyond his proper powers—or with regard to their form, if, though intended for the common good, their burdens should be inequitably distributed. Such laws come closer to violence than to true law ... They do not, therefore, oblige in conscience, except perhaps for the avoidance of scandal or disorder (*Summa Theologiæ*, I-II, 96, 4).

[139] See Aquinas:

The overthrow of such governments is not strictly sedition, unless perhaps when accompanied by such disorder that the community suffers greater harm than from the tyrannical government (*ibid.*, II-II, 42, 2).

destructive of will and reason. It may or may not even have certain short-term therapeutic merits. In so far as it is otherwise an unnatural act, it is no worse than coal mining. On Christian grounds, there is nothing to be said against it. It is an indifferent activity. On the matter of legislative control, those Christian advocates who are not merely putting a religious gloss on their secular views are guilty of a fundamental misconception—that it is the duty of government to make people good. It is the duty of government to do no such thing. It is instead to maintain an orderly environment in which we are able to do such good as we may choose of our own free will. If a Christian has any duty to become involved in politics, the politics appropriate to his faith are those of what used to be called liberalism, and which are today found in diluted form in the Conservative Party. If he has any duty to take a position on smoking, that position is surely one strongly opposed to any restrictions which have not as their end the protection of others. John Stuart Mill was not a Christian, but his words on liberty, properly construed, are fully in accord with Christianity. Though subject ultimately to God, where secular relationships are concerned, "[o]ver himself, over his own body and mind, the individual is sovereign".

3. THE RIGHT TO SMOKE:
A CONSERVATIVE VIEW

"Freedom is our most precious possession. To defend it and maintain it is no passive task, but one that requires continuous vigilance and resolve."
Margaret Thatcher[140]

I: The Risks of Smoking

That there are health hazards associated with smoking is probably true, although the wilder assertions of the anti-smoking lobby sometimes prompt one to wonder whether they have been exaggerated. However, there are health hazards associated with virtually every pleasurable human activity, and many whose pleasures escape me (pot-holing and hang–gliding, for example).

The majority of people in this country have been exposed to a massive campaign to alert them to the potential dangers of smoking and—as government surveys show fully accept the accuracy of those warnings.[141]

In spite of this, around two fifths of the adult British population still smoke. As a fraction of the whole, this has declined since the Fifties. But the most recent General Household Survey shows that 33 per cent of people smoke cigarettes.[142] Why? The British public is very

[140] Margaret Thatcher, *In Defence of Freedom: Speeches on Britain's Relations with the World 1976-1986*, Aurum Press, London, 1986, p.17.

[141] As an instance of this, consider the following In the December of 1983, David Simpson, Director of the pressure group Action on Smoking and Health (ASH), claimed that smoking had killed the last four Kings of Great Britain. Writing in *The Times* for the 22nd of that month, Bernard Levin held this claim up to ridicule, calling its author a "reckless and absurd" fanatic. Indeed, its sole justification appears to have been—first, that each of those Kings was an occasional smoker, and, second, that each is now dead. *Post hoc ergo propter hoc.*

[142] Figures quoted in H. Ashton & R Stepney, *Smoking Psychology and Pharmacology*, London, Tavistock Publications, 1983, p. 11.

far from stupid. It is one of the most stolid, level-headed groups of people in the world. What can make one third of it continue with an activity known at least to some extent to be harmful?

One proposed answer is that the big interests prefer things this way. The cigarette market worldwide is dominated by seven giant companies—rather, by seven multinationals! In this country alone they spend over £100 million a year on advertising; and governments are kept quiet by the scale of the revenue brought in. In 1987-88, for example, the United Kingdom government raised £5,775 million in excise duties and Value Added Tax from the sale of tobacco products.[143] It takes only a certain view of politics, and all the materials are there for a really big conspiracy theory.

Yet, all cigarette packets show the words "WARNING: SMOKING CAN CAUSE FATAL DISEASES Health Department's Chief Medical Advisers". Since their introduction in 1971, these health warnings have become increasingly lurid. They are also duplicated in Welsh where appropriate. To be sure, they may have become so familiar that no one takes the trouble to read them any more. Similarly, hoardings displaying cigarette adverts are identified beyond all doubt by the words printed bold in black on white just across them—"H.M. Government Health Warning: Cigarettes can seriously damage your health". The average smoker may not have read the detailed medical literature. He may avoid newspaper articles or television documentaries summarising it. He would need, even so, to be blind or illiterate not to have some basis for making an informed choice on whether or not to light up.

Another favourite answer is that cigarettes are so hugely addictive that most smokers, having once tasted them, are incapable of giving them up. "Once a smoker always a smoker" says the medical expert M. A. H. Russell.[144] Says he elsewhere: "[I]t requires no more than three or four casual cigarettes during adolescence virtually to ensure

---

[143] Written Answer, *Hansard*, 19th December, 1988, p. 28.

[144] *Guardian*, 31st March, 1977; quoted in Ashton & Stepney, *op. cit.*, p. 140.

that a person will eventually become a regular dependent smoker. Only about 15 percent of those who have more than one cigarette avoid becoming regular smokers."[145]

This, I suspect, is one of those exaggerations which do the case against smoking no service. From my own experience, Russell's claims sound unlikely; and they are easily questioned on better grounds than that. He admits himself that it requires around 20 cigarettes a day before physiological dependency becomes apparent.[146] In 1980, a quarter of current smokers claimed a daily consumption of ten cigarettes or less. 62 percent of women and 48 percent of men claimed one of less than twenty cigarettes.[147] By his own definitions, then, a good half of all smokers are not regularly dependent on their cigarettes. In the ten years from 1977, moreover, 20 percent of British smokers are believed to have given up the habit. [148] The evidence of a will-rotting addiction seems rather tenuous.

What, then, of the frequent claim that most smokers want to give up but are unable? Certainly, in a 1978 opinion poll, 41 percent of current smokers said not only that they did want to give up smoking, but that they had also tried and failed.[149] Other research, however, indicates that this desire should not be taken altogether seriously. In a study of 12,000 Philadelphian smokers, 41 percent of those questioned claimed an interest in giving up if help were available. A clinic was set up. It was made use of by just 150—or 3 per cent of the 41 per cent.[150] As those citing this ask with a common sense rare in

---

[145] Quoted *ibid*, p.140.

[146] *Ibid*, p. 141.

[147] *Ibid*, p. 141.

[148] Whitaker, *op. cit.*, p. 153.

[149] Ashton & Stepney, *op. cit.*, p. 141.

[150] *Ibid*, p. 142.

their field, 'how better for a smoker to avoid the pesterings of a physician or other interviewer than to say (whether believing it or not) that he wants to and has even tried to give up cigarettes?'.[151]

Then we have the Freudians—predictable as ever. People smoke, we are told, because a cigarette looks like a penis or a nipple. [152] Sometimes we are told it expresses parricidal intent.[153] Doubtless, the psychologists do have much to tell us that is both interesting and true, though many will find these particular claims far fetched. I might also say that, whatever explanation Freud himself favoured, he got through twenty cigars a day for most of his life.[154]

II: ... and the Benefits

In reality, people smoke for the same reason that they do most other things—because they believe doing it to give more pleasure than not doing it. And, as many smokers will admit in the right sort of company, cigarettes do give a lot of pleasure.

Try to imagine a smoker's first cigarette of the day. The act comprises very much more than a mere dragging away in search of a nicotine fix. There is the familiar procedure of unwrapping the packet, opening it, taking out the cigarette, followed by the rich, familiar smell of the tobacco as the filter is placed between the lips. Each brand is as individual as the different brands of coffee or tea. Each has its own texture, smell and taste. The range of variation is endless. It goes from the smoothest, mellowest Virginia, to those exotic, aromatic orientals, which only the most specialised palate can appreciate. With each perhaps is connected its own train of thought, recalling friends met, places visited, hopes realised or dashed. The sudden brightness of the flame illuminates the morning dullness. Then the smoke is

---

[151] *Ibid.*

[152] Whitaker, *op. cit.*, p.149.

[153] Ashton & Stepney, *op. cit.*, p. 25

[154] *Ibid*, p. 24.

drawn down into the lungs. From that first inhalation, it takes an average of seven seconds for the nicotine to be absorbed through the bronchioles into the bloodstream, and carried thence to the brain. Within seven seconds, the spell is working its effect on the smoker's mood. Nicotine stimulates. Nicotine soothes. It cheers the lonely. It aids the sociable. A pleasure in itself, it enhances every other. It came to Europe back with Columbus, and has been the valued friend of millions ever since.

Yet, considering this matter, of expense, it is worth noting that, whatever it may on the whole be, the balance in the case of individuals need not always be negative. Insofar as nicotine soothes the nerves, it may sometimes reduce the chance of stomach ulcers and other stress-related illnesses. It may prevent many suicides and perhaps the occasional murder.[155] Insofar as it depresses appetite, it restrains obesity and may sometimes lower rather than raise the chances of heart disease. Even otherwise—even if in every case it should be an expensive friend—to measure quality of life purely by duration needs a singular poverty of spirit. "Do you think ... it so very lucky to have a long miserable life?" asked Freud of his doctors when told to cut his smoking.[156]

Whether or not we ourselves share them, tobacco has very definite pleasures; and most of us nowadays do not share them—willingly recognise that they exist.

III: The Anti-Smoking Lobby

There are, nonetheless, individuals and groups who remain quite unmoved by this. First among these are many doctors. We all need their help at least occasionally; and it would be unnatural if they were not saddened or alarmed at some of the maladies we take before

---

[155] Whether or not smoking can ever be good for the health, giving up has certainly claimed at least one victim. There was an unfortunate lady in 1986, who stopped smoking, and promptly died of an asthma attack brought on by the resulting nervous agitation. See *The Times*, London, 17th October 1986.

[156] Ashton and Stepney, *op. cit.*, p.25.

them. Quite a few are wholly self-inflicted. Many others are worsened by what we do. If there were less smoking, they reason—and, I suppose, correctly enough—there would be less illness. If warnings have too little effect, some go on to reason next, some form of compulsion is in order. Few of them have gone on record as supposing that an activity so hugely popular as smoking still is could ever be prohibited outright. Even so, their final target can only seem to be the complete banning of tobacco. Their professional body, the British Medical Association, has been for some time now pressing for four preliminary measures of control. First, there is to be the phasing out of all advertising and sponsorship by the tobacco companies. Second, there is to be increasingly heavy taxation of all tobacco products. Third, there is to be the creation of civil law remedies for those who suffer by smoking. Fourth, the right to smoke in all public places is to be gradually taken away. These are so often and so publicly demanded that giving multiple examples would be a waste of paper. One is enough for all. In 1984, it was announced that black-lined cards were to be distributed to general practitioners, for sending to their Members of Parliament whenever any patient's death could be plausibly ascribed to his having smoked.[157]

Seconding in this campaign is the pressure group, Action on Smoking and Health. While this lacks the gravity and prestige of a chartered institution, it is equally less bounded by the constraints of truth and common sense; [158] and so, despite its small and unrepresentative membership, it counts in the media as an important interest.

Then there are many people in the Labour Party, wanting to save us from ourselves or whatever it believes is threatening us. Shortly before the last election its Health Spokesman, Frank Dobson,

---

[157] Reported in *The Times*, London, 13th November 1984. I have yet to receive one of these cards; but the publicity given the scheme might have been considered sufficient without going to the trouble of actually putting it into effect.

[158] See Note 2 above.

promised a total ban on tobacco advertising or promotion should it ever come to power again. [159] Ten days later, it published a consultative document in which was aired the possibility of forbidding all sponsorship by tobacco companies—but still forcing them to hand the money over as before, in case sporting events should suffer thereby any loss.[160]

IV: Conservatism: The Party of Freedom

For myself, I stand by the right to enjoy smoking. I am fiercely and unalterably opposed to any measures which will, for the sake of a smoker's own supposed benefit, tend to infringe that right. But then I am a Conservative. I belong to the Party of Freedom.

Now, since I am writing for a general audience, this assertion may raise a few sceptical smiles. There are, indeed, countries where to make it would be to state a contradiction. Throughout much of Europe, conservatism often means a fondness for the old authoritarian right. At times, it has meant something very different, and very much worse.

In the United Kingdom there is a main party of state in this country which has totalitarian leanings. Some of its more prominent members seem to want the violent overthrow of the present constitution. Some others gladly look forward to a reign of terror. That party is not the Conservative Party.

I turn now to the other misconceived view of what British Conservatism is—that it is a local variant of a European movement. Its advocates are blessed with an enviable clarity, and often with brilliance. Their attacks on the "cold hearts and muddy understandings" of the left, and exposure of its tyrannical leanings, have earned them a leading position in modern British thought. But

---

[159] *The Times*, London 20th January 1987.

[160] Reported in *The Times*, London, 30th January 1987. There is something splendidly ironic about the Party of the smoke-filled room solemnly discussing moves against the cigarette.

our native conservatism has nothing elaborately metaphysical about it. It subsists in a strong regard for custom and tradition, together with a dislike of unnecessarily rapid change. And, if anyone cares to ask what single principle our customs and traditions exemplify, the answer is easy: it is freedom.

The history of the British Isles, to an extent greater than in any other old country, has been the history of Freedom. It begins nearly eight hundred years ago, when a King was forced to concede for all time that in England the subject has certain rights, and that the law protecting them stands far above any mere holder of power.[161]Since 1215, this pledge has been ratified 37 times, most recently by Her Present Majesty at her Coronation in 1953.

Nearly every following event has been concerned with the working out or reaffirmation of this principle. The summoning of the first Parliament; Mr Justice Markham's sentencing of Prince Hal; the Petition of Right; the Bill of Rights; the Act of Settlement; Fox's Libel Act; Catholic Emancipation; the abolition of slavery; the Married Woman's Property Acts—these are just some of those events. Each one is a milestone in the progress of human liberty.

It is true that many of our currently enjoyed rights we owe to the Whigs and Liberals; and the Conservative Party, thinking them

---

[161] There is a copy of the *Magna Carta* on permanent display in the British Museum. Its Latin is not very classical, and its characters are hard to make out. But the 39th Article reads:

Nullus liber homo capiatur vel imprisonetur aut disseisietur aut utlagetur aut aliquo modo destruatur nec super eum ibimus nec super eum mittemus nisi per legale iudicium parium suorum vel per legem terr[a]e.

Roughly translated, this means:

Let no free man be arrested, or imprisoned, or deprived of his property, or outlawed, or by any other means harmed—neither will we go upon him, nor will we put upon him—except by the lawful judgment of his peers, or by the law of the land.

unwise or simply inopportune changes, was often on the wrong side of the question. But where are the Whigs and Liberals now? The Whigs entered the Conservative Party after 1886, bringing their traditions with them. The Liberals entered likewise after 1922. No matter how bitter the old disputes may have been, they have been ended by the fusion of the three parties into one. To see the truth of this, we need only look back over the past ten years of Conservative rule. Margaret Thatcher came to power in 1979 after a long period during which our old national emphasis on the individual had been giving way to what seemed a more exciting—even a more 'scientific'—trust in the collective. She set immediately to work. Her Government has since then done more to roll back the frontiers of the State than any other this century. It has given back to the people choice in education and in housing to a degree that only ten years ago would have been thought utopian. It is extending the same kind of choice in health. It has clearly affirmed the right to belong or not to belong to a trade union. It has stood up for the rights of British subjects in every part of the world. It has reduced the top rate of income tax from 98 per cent to 40 per cent, and the lower rate from 33 per cent to 25 per cent.

I believe that the process of setting the people free has many mountains to climb. Its timetable extends into the next century. It would be grossly inconsistent to take this general line, and at the same time demand or accept curbs on smoking. The Party of Freedom, to which I belong, should apply its principles consistently.

V: Individual Rights

I believe, like John Stuart Mill that

> the sole end for which mankind are warranted, individually or collectively, in interfering with the liberty of action of any of their number is self-protection .... [T]he only purpose for which power can be rightly exercised over any member of a civilised community, against his will, is to prevent harm to others. His own good, either physical or moral, is not a sufficient warrant. He cannot rightfully be compelled to do or forbear because it will be better for him to do so, because it will make him happier, because, in the opinion of others, to do so would be wise, or

even right .... Over himself, over his own body and mind, the individual is sovereign."162

So long as we commit no trespass against the life or property of another human being, how we use this sovereignty over ourselves is a matter for ourselves alone. It may be gathering as much money or status as can be legally had in a given time. It may be a life of self-sacrifice, helping the poor in the Third World. It may be risking life and liberty standing up for what is believed right. It may be smoking twenty cigarettes a day in spite of the known risks to health. But how one of us decides to spend his or her life is not a matter in which anyone else may rightly interfere. Each of us is different, and there is no one who can know in advance what it pleases us to do with ourselves. There are people who disagree with this. They watch others making choices which they themselves would not make, and grow distressed. They talk variously of "psychopathic personality disorders" or "false consciousness". Put whatever way pleases, all this talk reduces to is a claim to the running of someone else's life. Those from whom it issues are, to quote Churchill, "autocratic philanthropists who aspire to change the human heart as if by magic and make themselves our rulers at the same time".163

VI: Anti-Smoking and Anti-Democratic Elitisms

They are also, of course, anti-democrats. I know that freedom and democracy are not the same thing. The first answers the question of what powers the government should have, the second merely of by what right it should hold them. A government might be largely or even wholly unelected, and yet allow the widest personal freedom. At the same time, a democratic majority can easily be imagined voting its freedoms away. The old saying 'One man, one vote—once' is sad testimony to this.

Yet though freedom can exist perfectly well without democracy, there is no such thing as democracy without freedom. As Margaret

---

162 J. S. Mill *On Liberty*, *op. cit.*, pp. 72-3.

163 BBC Election Broadcast, reported in *The Times*, London, 22nd June 1945.

Thatcher has said "[a] belief in parliamentary democracy is incompatible with belief in the superior rights of any group, section or class over any other."[164] To say that people are incapable of running their own lives, and at the same time leave them free to run the lives of everyone else, is an absurd proposition and not one often applied. By an irony too common to notice, just about every unfree country calls itself a democracy. In every one of those countries, democracy is a sham. The whole moral grounding of the anti-smoking lobby is a belief that there is one group of people—doctors, puritans, or whatever—with a superior knowledge of what is good for everyone else. Whether or not this knowledge is superior, one thing is certain: to the extent that these people want to impose their belief on others, then their views are incompatible with the principles not only of freedom but of democracy.

VII: Smoking and Class Conflict

This would be the case if smokers were a group defined simply by their activity. It becomes so all the more if we realise that this—to borrow a phrase—is 'a class issue'. There can be few institutions in the country more solidly bourgeois than the British Medical Association. Action for Smoking and Health, though scarcely solid in any nattering sense, is clearly at least middle class—or so I judge by the accents of its leading members. Yet, to an increasing extent, smoking is an activity of the lower income groups. In 1972, 33 per cent of female professional workers smoked, by 1982, only 21 per cent. During the same period, the per centage of female unskilled workers who smoked fell by just one point, from 42 per cent to 41 per cent.[165] Cigarettes are fast disappearing from the average dinner party in Hampstead. On the housing estates, from South London to Glasgow, lighting up remains perfectly normal in company—as much a part of watching television as making tea during the commercial break.

---

[164] Thatcher, *op. cit.*, p. 16.

[165] M. A. Plant, *Drugs in Perspective*, Hodder *and* Stoughton, London, 1987, p. 69.

It is now 42 years since the Labour Party statesman Douglas Jay, wrote these words:

> ... [I]n the case of nutrition and health, just as in the case of education, the gentleman in Whitehall really does know better what is good for the people than the people know themselves."[166]

Since then, the voice of middle class bossiness has lost much of its glad, confident tone. The underlying ethos lives on even so.

VIII: Smoking and the Philosophic Case for Freedom

All this having been said, I turn now to the matter of whether any state-imposed restrictions on smoking can be regarded as entirely proper. In the first place, let us examine the grounds on which freedom is justified. For me, it consists in the simple wish that people should be as happy as they can be—or, failing this, no more unhappy than is absolutely inevitable. I believe that this state of affairs is best realised if people are left to their own choices, rather than if directed by some outside authority. Now, this belief is not open to direct verification. To say that economic freedom tends to make people rich is to state an empirically testable hypothesis; and its proof is for me the whole lesson of Economics. But happiness is not the same as wealth. I say that freedom tends to maximise happiness. But the implication of what I have already said is that what makes people happy is revealed by what they freely do. Therefore, any direct verification of the belief involves arguing in a circle: what people freely do makes them happy, because what makes them happy is shown by what they freely do.

What I must do, then, is state a further hypothesis in support—that

---

[166] Douglas Jay, *The Socialist Case*, Victor Gollancz, London, 1947, p. 258. Worth stressing here is that this was not some casual remark pounced on by a journalist and quoted out of context. It comes from the second revised edition of a book first published ten years previously, and is therefore the product of some consideration as to its meaning. There may be socialist libertarians. Jay was not one of them.

people are responsible agents. This is to say that, when making choices which are irrevocable or seen by others as self-destroying, they are presumed capable of understanding what they are doing. Take away this presumption of capacity, and freedom would be about as useful to them as a candle is to a blind man. This is testable. In most adults, we can easily see the capacity to exist, even where it is not often used. For example, imagine that I see a neighbour lean out of an upstairs window in his house to clean the glass. He is not wearing a harness. He leans back too far, and falls onto his front lawn. I run to help him, but he stands up shaken though unhurt. "Fixing a harness seemed a lot of trouble" he says. "I took a chance and lost." Alternatively, he says: "How dreadful that fall was. I never realised I might be in so much danger." In either case, I assess his degree of present responsibility from observed or inferred past conjunctions of desire and outcome. Assume that I do find him responsible, and in the first case nothing much need be said: he made a miscalculation. In the second, I can only shake my head and wonder at a grown man being so careless. If I see him coughing his heart up over a cigarette, precisely the same reasoning applies.

Children, on the other hand, are different. The capacity for making an informed choice exists in them only potentially. It becomes actual with time and the gaining of experience. Until then, there is no virtue in treating them as free. Insofar as smoking cigarettes involves very probable dangers to health, they should be kept out of the hands of children. The only room for argument here is over means rather than ends. Control should be enforced ideally by the parents. But if they refuse or are too weak to do this, I see a perfectly legitimate role for the State. The Protection of Children (Tobacco) Act 1986 is only the most recent declaration that this role has been assumed.

For the same reason, I am inclined to say the same regarding those adults found suffering from such evident defects of reason as to be judged incapable of making any other choices for themselves. Naturally, I am cautious on this point. For reasons too obvious to set out, I believe that the normal presumption with adults should be of responsibility, and that any exemption from this should be made on specific application, and only in the light of clear evidence. But, where clear evidence is found, a case for denying the right to smoke

131

does exist.

IX: "Externalities" and the Alleged Grounds for Restricting Liberty

Moving on from this, I now discuss the possibility of restrictions for the sake of protecting the rights of others. Here, a moral victory has been gained against the anti-smoking lobby. For years, not just the main, but usually the sole, argument was that tobacco harmed the smoker. In our own age of reviving individualism, this is no longer thought enough. Increasingly, the emphasis is shifting to the alleged harm suffered by third parties. To the extent that this shift is taking place, a vital point is being silently conceded—that what people do to themselves is no one else's business. As for the new kinds of claim advanced, these are, in the absence of decent evidence, fairly easily dealt with.

i: The NHS and the Costs of Smoking

First, there is the claim that the treatment of diseases related to smoking is an expense to the whole community. In 1984, the medical cost was assessed at £370 million.[167] Evidently, money spent on one thing cannot be spent on something else; and, mindful of this, at least one doctor has refused to give his time and the resources at his disposal to anyone who will not stop smoking.[168] £370 million is a lot of money to spend on treating what some would call self-made invalids. But the £5,775 million tax harvest raised from smoking in 1987-88 is a lot more money—some thirteen and a half times more. So far from being a strain on the National Health Service, smokers pay their own way—and pay it pretty handsomely.

Simple arithmetic refutes this particular argument. But, even assuming the financial balance were entirely reversed, it would still be worth resisting. It contains a principle which, established in any one respect, would logically entail the most searching state control over

---

[167] *The Times*, London, 30th January 1987.

[168] *The Times*, London, 14th January 1987.

our lives. For, unless a relationship of master and slave be intended, every right granted and obligation conferred carries its own limiting reciprocal. Oblige me, for example, to keep a child out of harm, and I must have the right to stop him from playing with fire. Oblige me to keep him healthy, and I must have the right to stop him from drinking bleach. Oblige me to educate him, and I must have the right to compel his attendance at the appropriate place of learning. Give him the right to my protection, and oblige him at the same time to obey me in doing what I think for his good.

Now, it does seem that the National Health Service, as currently funded, implies a relationship of exactly this kind. Those of us who pay National Insurance Contributions might well be entitled to wonder if we have not the same unlimited obligation on us that a slave owes to his master. This being found so, and it being assumed that smokers were a net burden on the system, it would only be common justice if we looked round for some limiting reciprocal. It would be a public right then to put curbs on smoking, even to the extent of an outright ban. By the same reasoning, however, any other activity—no matter how traditional or how honoured, or, for that matter, how private—from which a danger to health significantly above average were found to result, would be equally open to control.

It says much in favour of the British public that this argument has never been seriously advanced or considered. Logical consistency is a fine thing. Common sense is better every time. But the danger is there. In the long term, given the reforms already being carried through by Kenneth Clarke in the Department of Health, it will diminish, as private money becomes increasingly merged with state provision. For the moment, any version of the argument should be resisted whenever heard.

ii: The Alleged Effects of "Passive Smoking"

The second claim is that smokers pollute the air, so exposing non-smokers about them to all the health risks associated with tobacco. According to one Japanese study, "the deleterious effects of passive smoking may occur in proportion to the exposure of non-smokers to smokers in the home, the workplace, and the community."[169] Perhaps 50 per cent of non-smokers living in cities are thought to have absorbed significant amounts of nicotine into their bloodstreams from the surrounding air.[170] In another Japanese study, it is alleged that non-smoking women with smoking husbands are twice as likely to develop lung cancer as those with non-smoking husbands.[171]

This is an extremely serious claim. If ever established, it would at once shift all debate from whether anything should be done about smoking to what should be done. Not surprisingly, therefore, the concept of "passive smoking" has been taken up with enthusiasm, and proclaimed as an established fact. For the moment, it remains nothing of the sort. Other studies have found no statistical correlations anywhere near so certain as those found in Japan. In one of them, for example, levels of nicotine in the air were checked at 47 offices and 48 restaurants. The conclusion reached was that it would take an average of 550 hours seated at a desk and of 400 hours seated at a table before enough nicotine would be absorbed equivalent to having smoked one cigarette.[172] The evidence for passive smoking remains so ambiguous that no definite conclusions can as yet be drawn from it. Those which are drawn are often pure fabrication. In 1986, the Surgeon General of the United States went on record as stating that 2,000 American adults died each year as a result of passive smoking. When challenged to prove this, he retracted the statement, claiming that, if untrue, it had still been made in a good cause.[173]

Even if, moreover, a definite correlation ever were found, it would

---

[169] Quoted Whitaker, *op. cit.*, p. 151.

[170]*Ibid*, p. 152.

[171]*Ibid.*

[172] *The Times*, London, 13th March 1987.

[173] *Ibid.*

still not automatically follow that government action were required. For a solution to be worth adopting, it must first be shown both likely to work and not likely to result in the creation of fresh and unacceptable problems elsewhere. Our experience generally of government action has not been encouraging. When action is to be considered against a pleasure enjoyed by millions, our only available experience indicates that it might be disastrous. I am thinking of the American alcohol prohibition. This had its optimistic advocates, promising heaven on earth if only something were stamped on hard enough. Said the evangelist Billy Sunday when they had their way in 1920: "The reign of tears is over. The slums will soon only be a memory. We will turn our prisons into factories and our jails into storehouses and corn cribs. Men will walk upright now, women will smile, and the children will laugh. Hell will be forever for rent."[174] By 1930, over half a million Americans had been arrested for alcohol offences. Another 35,000 had died of alcohol poisoning. [175] Organised crime and public corruption had become endemic in the United States, and have remained so ever since. Of course, as said above, no respectable group or individual has yet come openly out in favour of tobacco prohibition. But the American example illustrates as plainly as anything ever can that government action does not always achieve its stated ends without a pretty high cost—and sometimes fails to achieve them at all. This said even so, let it be assumed, for the sake of argument, that a definite correlation were actually found to exist; and, the 'passive smoking' claims substantially verified, that smoking did carry a certain risk to third parties. This done, let us then look at the four main options for control earlier mentioned.

X: Smoking Restrictions: A Critique

i: Advertising and Free Speech

First, there are restrictions on the advertising of tobacco products.

---

[174] Quoted in Friedman (1972), p. 160.

[175] Whitaker, *op. cit.*, p. 137.

There are some opponents of these who claim that they would have no effect: people would go on smoking exactly as before. The argument is advertising results in consumers switching between brands, rather than affecting the total level of smoking. On the other side it has been argued that when a ban was imposed in Norway some years ago, smoking among young people there subsequently fell.[176] I prefer to stand on the fundamental grounds of opposition. Whatever the effect to which advertising restrictions work, it is clear that they constitute censorship.

Where political discussion is concerned, the case for free speech hardly needs putting. Introduce the power of government onto either side of a dispute, and, as Macaulay said, "instead of a contest between argument and argument, we have a contest between argument and force. Instead of a contest in which truth, from the natural constitution of the human mind, has a decided advantage over falsehood, we have a contest in which truth can be victorious only by accident."[177]

This is true for politics, and I see no reason why it should not be equally true for other kinds of discussion. Except they urge different actions, the statements "Vote for X" and "Smoke Y" fall into exactly the same class. Both recommend people to do a certain thing. Both, if amplified, will have reasons attached for doing so. The reasons given may be good or bad. The politician may be a corrupt egomaniac. The cigarettes may be almost dripping tar. Both statements, if acted on to a sufficiently large extent, might result in varying degrees of harm to the community. Suppressing either

---

[176] *The Times*, London, 15th August 1986. Not surprisingly the anti-smokers have actually distorted the evidence regarding the Norwegian case. Smoking had been steadily declining there anyway. The advertising ban produced no significant change in this decline, either way. Indeed, there have been greater decreases in **smoking** in countries without bans—like Britain—and no decreases in countries with bans or partial bans. See Michael J. Waterson, *Advertising and Cigarette Consumption*, Advertising Association, London, 1984.

[177] T. B. Macaulay, *Critical and Historical Essays* (1844), Everyman Books, J. M. Dent, London, 1909, vol. 2, p. 209.

involves an attack on the free communication of ideas, and, as such, on the efficient separation of truth from falsehood.

Though there are as yet no legal restrictions in this country on advertising or promotion of tobacco products, there is an agreement between the government and the tobacco companies. This is supervised by the Advertising Standards Authority. From the continual and bitter railing against it by the anti-smoking campaigners,[178] it might be thought that this had no effect, and that it certainly fell short of censorship. But restrictive agreements to which a government is one party and some of its subjects the other are seldom voluntary except in form; and this agreement seems not only to constitute censorship, but censorship of a rather dangerous sort.

In early 1987, the parties met for the purpose of setting further regulations of advertising at sports events sponsored by the tobacco companies. The result of this meeting was that the amount of sponsorship money given to explicit advertising was cut from 30 per cent to 20 per cent, and the size of the Government Health Warning on the advertisements was increased by 50 per cent, to 15 per cent of the total size.[179] To call this sort of agreement "voluntary" is an almost Orwellian misuse of language. What we have here instead is surely an instance of what Enoch Powell some twenty years ago called the "Rule of the Threat of Law".[180] A government wants something done, yet feels disinclined to trouble with changing the law to compel that thing's doing. So it announces its wish and invites the "voluntary compliance" of those to be affected—who, of course, do comply, through fear of indirect consequences if they refuse or of an eventual regular law which might be more onerous. There is no guiding of a bill through the two houses, no explaining or giving of

---

[178] See, for example, the comments reported in *The Times*, 20th January 1987.

[179] *Ibid.*

[180] Enoch Powell, *Freedom and Reality*, Elliot Right Way Books, Kingswood, Surrey, 1969, p. 133 *et passim*. See also Ulpian's slavish maxim: "*quod principi placuit legis vigorem habet*".

reasons, no question of appeal to the Courts by anyone who might think himself harmed. Since there is no actual law, there is no bar on selective indulgences or victimisations. There are simply the words of those in power "Let this be done" and it is done.

Any country in which this is allowed to become a normal and accepted mode of government has lost its freedom. Regular elections may still be held. The Judges may retain their independence. But when the principle has gone out of a Constitution—that there is no authority outside that given by law—the line dividing freedom from serfdom has been crossed.

Applied to the situation in Great Britain today, this of course sounds grossly alarmist. So far from going down the road to serfdom, we turned resolutely back up it in 1979, and have been moving further away from it ever since. On one point, I stand squarely with the anti-smoking lobby: the Voluntary Agreement must go. I see no good reason why the tobacco industry should be treated any differently from any other industry in a free market.

ii: The Counter-Productive Effect of High Tobacco Taxation

Second, there is heavier taxation of tobacco products, thereby raising prices. The advocates of this scheme often like to present their case in the technical language of economics. They draw graphs, purporting to show how every fresh two pence or whatever on a packet of twenty will cut smoking by so many millions. [181] Economists may be growing increasingly sceptical of whether demand schedules can ever be drawn for a real world of constantly shifting tastes. I suspect that the real purpose of all this calculating and plotting is largely to impress people with the scientific truth of the argument being advanced, as well as its alleged justice. I see no reason, however, to doubt its basic premise. The higher the price of a good, generally speaking and other things being equal, the smaller will be the quantity of it bought. Demand for cigarettes appears to be fairly inelastic, much the same number being bought at any price tried

---

[181] See, as an example of this the Study of A. B. Atkinson & J. L. Townsend, summarised in Ashton and Stepney, *op. cit.*, p. 146.

so far. But it seems quite evident that, prices being pushed far enough, there would be a substantial fall in demand. All the same, I can think of several perhaps fundamental objections.

There is the effect on the public finances. This is, I know, its third mention; but £5,775 million is a lot of money. If taxes were increased far beyond whatever point at which net revenues began to decline, greater burdens would need to be placed elsewhere. At the moment, the public sector is in massive surplus. The burden probably could be shifted with little apparent effort. It should be remembered, though, that this is the first government in the better part of a generation able to finance all its spending while at the same time remaining solvent. Quite a few of those who cry out for depressive taxation on tobacco also cry out against the only policies which make it even half possible. Long may they never be forced to reconcile these cries!

There is our membership of the European Community. We are committed to an eventual harmonisation of taxes. This might involve cigarette prices in Greece and Portugal rising from their current average of 50p per packet of twenty. It would certainly be incompatible With prices in Britain remaining at their present level, let alone being pushed higher.

Then there is the "class issue" again. For those smokers in the higher income groups, cigarettes could probably rise from 6p to 50p each; and there would be grumblings and frettings, and consumption would go on much as before. For those in the lower income groups, it would be a tremendous burden—and rightly seen as an unfair one. It would, moreover, give them a decided incentive to smoke each cigarette right down to the butt, where we are told the greatest concentration of toxic substances is to be found. It seems very likely that one of the most impressive effects of higher taxes would be an unequal incidence of smoking-related illnesses between the smokers of different income groups.

If these were the only unintended consequences of increased taxation, they might be sufficient in themselves to damn the whole scheme. But after a certain point, high taxation becomes wholly counter-productive. Taxes at any level could be levied on the tobacco sold out of the bonded warehouses. But, eventually the effects of prices made artificially high would begin to imitate those of an outright prohibition. There would be smuggling and illicit home production on a large scale, with all that means for crime, corruption and the customary restraints on use which now keep people from immoderate indulgence. In short, features which characterized the whole sad history of American alcohol prohibition would be repeated right here in Great Britain with tobacco.

iii: Should Tobacco Companies Be Liable for Civil Damages?

Third, there is the imposition on the tobacco companies of civil law liability for any damages caused by smoking. Now, a distinction of vital importance must be drawn here. As a Conservative, I believe that disputes are best settled when left as far as possible to the adjudication of the ordinary Courts. There is a subtlety and individuality of regard for circumstances in the application of case law that a general statute can never begin to match. Take, for example, this Government's trade union reforms. Every previous attempt at bringing the unions within the law had failed. It was not for want of determination that they failed—though, I confess, this was ultimately lacking. It was because the means used were too crude. Rules of conduct were announced, and then imposed on the parties to a dispute, whether or not either wanted to follow them. The Prior and Tebbit Acts imposed nothing. They merely enabled the traditional remedies of our legal system to be sought against a hitherto privileged group. If a union today calls a strike without first holding a ballot, or sends out gangs of secondary pickets, nothing happens except by request of one of the parties. An Action is begun for damages. Interlocutory injunctions are sought. The matter is argued before a Judge, or terms of compromise agreed. That is all. Yet the success of these reforms has become self-evident. We are in the eighth year of sustained economic growth. Unemployment is falling speedily and steadily. This, and relations between management and unions are more harmonious than at any time within living memory.

Following this precedent, I would go further, and suggest that many other current problems could be solved in the same way. Industrial pollution worries me as much as it does many 'Green' activists. We often differ only in what we believe should be done about it. They seem mostly to want fresh anti-pollution laws, to be enforced by Government-appointed inspectors. My preference is for the acknowledgement that individuals have rights to clean air and water, and the extension of common law remedies to their enforcement.

Being no lawyer, I am naturally cautious when it comes to any discussion of jurisprudence. But I believe that what I want is no more than the application of old principles in new circumstances. What the anti-smoking lobby wants seems altogether different. Without naming individual cases, it is trying to assert the right of a smoker to contract any of the illnesses associated with tobacco, and then sue for damages. To me, this appears to breach a central principle of the law of torts—that where there is consent to injury, there can be no cause for action.[182]

Consider: I come into your house. In there, I pick up a bottle which is clearly labelled "Poison". You tell me "Don't drink that. It's dangerous." I hear you, but drain the bottle, and go down in a fit. To say that I—or my next of kin—should be able to sue you for damages on account of this would be completely absurd. I should be so much the author of my own distress that the laws against suicide would once have applied to me. The case is surely an exact analogy of smoking. The apparent dangers are widely advertised. Every packet carries a warning. Any responsible adult who smokes nevertheless, and is later diagnosed as suffering from heart disease or lung cancer or whatever, has every right to feel upset, but none to a remedy at law against a tobacco company. Consent may not have been explicit. The words "I don't mind shortening my life" may not have been uttered. But that consent is as evidently given as though it had been expressed by formal deed. Certainly, anyone whose cigar explodes, or in whose pipe tobacco shredded asbestos is found, should have a remedy. These are not among the advertised dangers of smoking. Here, the smoker cannot be said to have consented to injury. But these cases fall within an entirely different class.

Nor can it save the argument to say that tobacco is addictive, and that

---

[182] "*Uolenti non fit iniuria*".

those smoking it, even if aware of the dangers, are unable to stop. In the first place, I have already indicated my doubts that smokers are as heavily addicted as is often claimed. In the second, even allowing that the fullest degree of addiction ever claimed might exist is only to shift the grounds of objection, not to change their validity. It is now at least thirty five years since the more serious medical warnings began to appear. Those who have started smoking since then have consented to their "addiction", and thereby to any subsequent effects. Those who began before then have had quite long enough to consider seeking assistance to break their habit, and, by not having sought assistance, have consented equally to whatever effects might follow. In fact, I should add that the concept of "addiction" is a very problematic one, certainly in the way it is popularly conceived, an habituation.[183]

For some, what I am saying may seem hard and uncaring. Some might think that I have a special fondness for the tobacco industry. I have none—or no more, at least, than I have for any other. As for being hard, I do feel the deepest personal sympathy for anyone who is dying or in pain. This is an absolute sympathy, given without regard to how the suffering may have been caused. But, on this point of legal liability, I fail to see how one person or group of persons can be blamed for the self-inflicted ills of another without an utter denial of human responsibility. And, as I have argued above, where there is no responsibility, there is no argument for freedom. A shape cannot at the same time be a square and a triangle. A person cannot at the same time be an adult and a child.

iv: Restrictions on Public Smoking

Fourth, there are progressively severe restrictions on smoking in public places. Whether or not non-smokers are in any real danger, no one can deny that they often find smoke-filled rooms uncomfortable or offensive. Anyone with a chest complaint, indeed, is very likely to suffer immediate, if perhaps short-term harm. It seems only reasonable that there should be some places where smoking is not

---

[183] See Jara Krivanek, *Addictions*, Allen and Unwin, London, 1988.

allowed—or rather, bearing in mind who the majority now are, to where smoking is confined. No one can object to a degree of separation.

Again, however, there is a distinction here to be drawn. What the anti-smoking lobby wants is compulsory restrictions. The model is the Californian 'Proposition Thirteen', a measure voted on by referendum in 1978. If accepted, this would have prohibited smoking by law in a great many places open to the public. The prohibition was to apply whether or not the owners or operators of those places wanted it, or whether or not those using them wanted it. The proposition was rejected. I am certain that any similar referendum in this country would go the same way. This particular violation of rights could only be enforced after an equal violation of democracy.

But, of course, there are restrictions on smoking, and these are becoming more complete. There are at the moment theatres, cinemas, buses, trains and so forth which are divided into smoking and non-smoking areas. In some places of work and in certain shops, and on the London Underground, smoking is altogether prohibited. These controls, if sometimes imposed by government bodies are a product of voluntary choice. They were imposed by the owners or operators in response to what they considered consumer preferences to be, and are enforced by them. They are a product of the free market. As such, they are entirely unobjectionable. A restauranteur has as much right to hang a 'No Smoking' sign inside his door as any other property owner has. Someone may feel put upon if not allowed to light a cigarette there after a meal, but, so long as the sign was on reasonably prominent display, has no right to complain; and, while two fifths of the population still enjoy smoking, there need be no shortage of restaurants where it is freely allowed. By the same reasoning, there need be no shortage—assuming a genuine demand—for any other place of business, travel or entertainment where smoking is or is not permitted.

XI: Conclusions

What I have, in these pages, sought to argue is that to attack the right to smoke is necessarily to attack the freedoms for which our ancestors fought and suffered. It is also to show contempt for a system of government which—in spite of all its admitted faults—has been a model for half the world and is the present hopeless envy of the other half. I honestly doubt whether the right of one person to smoke infringes the right of another to enjoy a healthy life. But I have, nonetheless, assumed that this might indeed be the case, and have examined the variously canvassed solutions. Every one of them that depends on government coercion I have shown either to be useless or to be accompanied by unsupportable general costs. The only one that is likely to succeed relies on that spontaneous coordination of individual choices that is called the free market. Examine any problem, real or illusory, and, if the cause is freedom, its solution in nearly every case will be more freedom.

The great French economist Frederic Bastiat made this very point repeatedly, and with great force and elegance. I might conclude by quoting him. Instead, I will simply follow his example, and quote the conservative writer Chateaubriand:

> There are two consequences in history: one immediate and instantaneously recognized; the other distant and unperceived at first. These consequences often contradict each other; the former comes from our short-run wisdom, the latter from our long-run wisdom. The providential event appears after the human event. Behind men rises God. Deny as much as you wish the Supreme Wisdom, do not believe in its action, dispute over words, call what the common man calls Providence 'the force of circumstances' or 'reason'; but look to the end of an accomplished fact, and you will see that it has always produced the opposite of what was expected when it has not been founded from the first on morality and justice.[184]

---

[184] From *Mémoires d'outre Tombe*, quoted in F. Bastiat, *Selected Essays on Political Economy*, trans. Seymour Cain, The Foundation for Economic Education, New York, 1975, pp.49-50.

4. COMMERCIAL ADVERTISING:
A THREATENED HUMAN RIGHT

Introduction

Advertising has long been regarded with a certain contempt in England. Those who get their money by it may not have been classed so low as pornographers and writers of begging letters. They have nonetheless been despised. In the eighteenth century, they were already unpopular enough to be satirised. Sheridan brought few characters onto the stage so grotesque as the cynical copywriter, Puff. He introduces himself:

> ...I love to be frank on the subject, and to advertise my self *viva voce.*—I am, sir, a practitioner in panegyric, or, to speak more plainly, a professor of the art of puffing, at your service—or anyone else's.[185]

In the next century, Macaulay began one of his reviews with an attack on the advertising of books:

---

[185] Richard Brinsley Sheridan, *The Critic: or a Tragedy Rehearsed* (1779), Act I, Scene II. Puff continues:

> Even the auctioneers now—the auctioneers, I say—though the rogues have lately got some credit for their language—not an article of merit theirs: take them out of their pulpits, and they are as dull as catalogues!—No, sir; 'twas I first enriched their style—'twas I first taught them to crowd their advertisements with panegyrical superlatives, each epithet rising above the other, like the bidders in their own auction rooms! From me they learned to inlay their phraseology with variegated chips of exotic metaphor: by me too their inventive were called forth:- yes, sir, by me they were instructed to clothe ideal walls with gratuitous fruits—to insinuate obsequious rivulets into visionary groves—to teach courteous shrubs to nod their approbation of the grateful soil; or on emergencies to raise upstart oaks where their never had been an acorn; to create a delightful vicinage without the assistance of a neighbour; or to fix the temple of Hygeia in the fens of Lincolnshire! (*ibid*).

...[H]ow any man who has the least self-respect, the least regard for his own personal dignity, can condescend to persecute the public with this Rag-fair importunity, we do not understand. Extreme poverty may, indeed, in some degree, be an excuse for stealing a leg of mutton. But we really think that a man of spirit and delicacy would quite as soon satisfy his wants in the one way as in the other.[186]

In our own century, advertising has grown into an enormous business. The old individual puffer has vanished, his place taken by agencies that are often household names throughout the world. They employ thousands. Their products are seen by millions and tens of millions. But the old prejudice continues. Advertisers are still blamed for their alleged venality. Every sign, real or imagined, of their philistine ignorance is held up for the public derision. Would the Saatchi brothers, for example, ever have found their way into *Private Eye* had they made their fortunes in chemicals or house building?

The prejudice continues—with an addition. There are people nowadays whose dislike of advertising does not end with their sneering at it. They want to control it. They believe that, so far from being a vulgar annoyance, it has a malign and often unperceived power over us that must be fought and overcome if we are to regain the direction of our own lives. All advertising they would see regulated by the authorities. Some they would see entirely banned.

Now, I propose here to examine what is implied in this regulation of advertising—from what view of human nature its proceeds; what further policies it may require. If I concentrate on the health activists to the relative exclusion of other groups in favour of regulation, it will not be on account of any specific personal or financial interest. It will, indeed, be paying them a deserved compliment. They are by far the most able and articulate enemies of unregulated advertising. Their arguments have been clearly stated to the public, and have been endorsed by many leading members of the medical profession. In consequence, they have been the most successful. They have been

---

[186] Thomas Babington Macaulay, *Essays, op. cit.*, review of Robert Montgomerey's *Poems* (1830) Vol. 2, p. 647.

taken more seriously by the political class than any other group. They seem much fairer set to having their way.

Again, if within the health activists, I give more attention to the anti-tobacco than to the anti-sugar or anti-pesticide lobbies, that also is because of its greater success to date. I will, of course, mention those feminists and others whose voices are from time to time raised against advertising. But their obscurity, their incoherence, their internal divisions, and their lack of practical success will surely excuse my not giving them the same attention as the health activists.

I: The Attack on Advertising

i: The Health Activists

The health activists share with the health educators—and indeed with most people—a very laudable wish. This is that we should all live as long as possible and remain as healthy as possible. They have firm ideas about what lifestyle is most appropriate for realising these goals, and have devoted their careers—often at large, and increasing, public expense—to persuading us to adopt that lifestyle. They want us to give up smoking, to drink less, and to change our diet.

On the whole, we have accepted their advice. Fewer cigarettes are smoked now than 15 years ago. Less alcohol is drunk.[187] More fibre is eaten, together with less fat and salt and sugar. But persuasion, much as it has achieved, is not enough. The health educators may be content to continue persuading us, trying to refute the objections raised against their advice, warning us against the temptations offered by those with a financial or some other interest in keeping us or bringing us back to the slovenly habits of our parents and grandparents. The health activists are less modest. They want to

---

[187] Since this is routinely denied by the anti-alcohol lobby, I refer the reader to M.J. Waterson, Advertising and Alcohol: A Review of the Evidence, in Digby Anderson (ed), *Drinking to Your Health: The Allegations and the Evidence*, The Social Affairs Unit, London, 1989, pp. 90-117. Measuring consumption in litres of 100 per cent pure alcohol, we drank 9.44 litres per head in 1978, and 9.13 litres in 1987—p. 96. Compare this with the 13.2 litres per head drunk in France in 1986, and the 10.5 in West Germany—p. 99.

enlist the coercive power of the State to propagating their message.

In 1988, a book appeared that can reasonably be regarded as a comprehensive statement of the activist orthodoxy. It was compiled by "an Independent Multidisciplinary Committee" on which every main activist lobby is represented. It was sponsored by the main bodies that dispense public funds to them.[188] Its authors accept that continued free persuasion has its place. But, they say,

> [i]t is also increasingly being recognised that human behaviour does not reflect individual choices alone so much as the powerful influence of the social, economic and political environments that lie substantially beyond the control of the individuals who are affected by them.[189]

There is a case, as they see it, for having the State guide us in our choices. It is to increase the taxes on tobacco and alcohol and whatever foods are currently thought bad for us, until we buy less of them. It is to subsidise more acceptable alternatives. [190] "[t]he provision of a wider variety of cheap non-alcoholic drinks (which at present are often overpriced)". It is to regulate methods of manufacture. It is to give much more money to the health activists. At the same time, it is to take and use sweeping powers to suppress those adverts that are deemed to promote an unhealthy lifestyle. This last is particularly important, for

---

[188] Alweyn Smith & Bobbie Jacobson (eds.), *The Nation's Health: A Strategy for the 1990s*. a Report from an Independent Multidisciplinary Committee Chaired by Professor Alweyn Smith, King Edward's Hospital Fund for London, London, 1988. The Sponsors were: The Health Education Council (to April 1987), The Health Education Authority (from April 1987), King Edward's Hospital Fund for London, The London School of Hygiene and Tropical Medicine, The Scottish Health Education Group.

[189] *Ibid.,* p.2.

[190] *Ibid,* p. 83, p. 91. In the first of these, the authors are discussing food and the five "broad strategies" for changing our diet. There is to be a pricing policy "to assist in the switch from harmful to healthy food".

human societies are often manipulated by some individuals to the risk of others. It is one of the functions of government to regulate such manipulation in both the best interests of collectivity and of its individual members.[191]

Food and drink adverts are merely to be regulated. There is to be less advertising of sweets, and less "misleading" persuasion of women to beautify themselves by cutting down on starchy foods.[192] For drink, there is to be a strict code, to prevent the making of any association of alcohol with "glamour or sexual prowess".[193] There is, in addition, to be a kind of negative advertising. At the moment, the food and drink manufacturers are able to tell us how good something will make us feel or look. They are not required to put us off buying it by telling us what it contains. This is to be remedied thus:

> The Ministry of Agriculture, Fisheries and Foods (MAFF) should implement a comprehensive food labelling system which clearly informs the consumer of the fat (saturated and unsaturated), sugar, fibre and salt content of all foods. A simple 'traffic lights' system of identifying foods that are high, medium or low in the above substances should be adopted.[194]

Similar requirements are imposed at the moment on the cigarette manufacturers. They are compelled to put us off their products by printing the most alarming warnings on the wrappers and adverts. In spite of this, though, there is to be no tobacco advertising. That is to be prohibited by law. It may be suitable with other things to "promote healthy, safe and enjoyable patterns of use or consumption".[195] But tobacco is unique. Cigarettes, says Nigel Smith

---

[191] *Ibid.*, p.4.

[192] *Ibid*, p. 85. See also *infra*, regarding the feminist claims.

[193] *Ibid*, p. 248.

[194] *Ibid*, pp. 243-44.

[195] *Ibid*, p. 77.

of the Health Education Authority, are

> the only product on the market in this country which kill
> people if they are used in the way the manufacturer intends.
> One in four people who regularly use cigarettes are going to die
> from a disease caused by their smoking....

> Advertising the product creates a climate in which smoking, in
> which tobacco seems to be respectable. It gives it an air of
> credibility which it should not have....

> [I]t's absolutely essential that in Britain there is a total ban of all
> advertising, all promotion, all sponsorship, not just of
> cigarettes but of any product which bears the image or bears
> the name of a cigarette.[196]

The State raises more than £6000 million each year—or about three
per cent of its total revenue—from the tobacco industry in excise
duties and value added tax. Even so, it would be surprising if these
bitter denunciations had been wholly ineffective. Since, it has been
illegal to advertise cigarettes on television. In 1970, while Sir Keith
Joseph was Minister of Health, the first of the "voluntary
agreements" was signed between his Ministry and the tobacco
industry. These were intended to regulate advertising without the
need for actual legislation. Periodically renewed and amended, they
have continued ever since. The latest version, due to expire in the
September of 1991—when it will be replaced by something still more
stringent—contains the following new provisions:

> * That the advertising of cigarettes in cinemas should cease;

> * That in place of the old health warnings, there should be six
> new warnings, to alternate and be ascribed to the Health
> Department's Chief Medical Officers;

---

[196] British Satellite Broadcasting, 5 pm, 28th May 1990—from a studio debate,
chaired by Jackie Spreckley, with Brendan Brady of the Tobacco Advisory
Council.

* That the space provided for health warnings and tar ratings on posters and press advertisements should be increased from 15 per cent to 17.5 per cent of the available area;[197]

* That spending on poster advertising should be frozen in real terms at 50 per cent of that for the year ending the 31st of March 1980;

* That no cigarette yielding more than 18mg of tar should be advertised.

* That no cigarette advertisements should appear in any magazine with a female readership of more than 200,000, of whom a third of more were aged between 15 and 24.[198]

But these agreements have always been denounced by the health activists as substitutes for real action. David Pollock, the Director of Action on Smoking and Health (ASH)—a charity set up in 1971 by the Royal College of Physicians, but now largely financed by the taxpayer—is predictably scornful:

> So long as the Government continues to rely on cosy agreements with the tobacco industry, they will condemn hundreds of thousands of British men and women to disease and early death.[199]

During the past few years, for all the zeal shown by individual Ministers, hopes of having the British Government do anything really effective have been abandoned. Since the passing of the Single European Act in 1986, hope has been largely transferred from London to Brussels. Before dealing with their success there, however,

---

[197] This had already risen under the previous Agreement from 10 per cent.

[198] Taken from Press Release 86/96, issued 24th March 1986 by the Department of Health and Social Security.

[199] "Smoking is cut" by bans on tobacco promotion, *The Daily Telegraph*, London, 6th September 1991.

I turn first to the feminists and other groups demanding the regulation of advertising.

ii: The Feminists and Others

To be sure, not all feminists are against advertising—or, indeed, call for more than the just legal equality of women. These have my total support and admiration. But there are certain feminists who go further, and seek liberation in some vague collectivist utopia. These regard the use of attractive women in adverts as part of the "patriarchal hegemonic discourse" which they must smash before they can be truly liberated. For them, advertising "commodifies" the female body, denying women their status as human beings. It constructs images

> purely from a male viewpoint, reinforcing the already unequal power relationship between men and women in society and simultaneously producing norms for women to aspire to. Much of the gratuitous use of the female body in advertising suggests that all women are available anytime to men.[200]

Advertising is said also to help keep women in their place. According to Naomi Wolf, the political and economic gains of the past generation are checked by keeping women hungry. Emancipation has been frozen by the cult of thinness. Recommended body weights have been reduced for women. Conformity to these is encouraged by the continual association in the media—and especially in adverts—of beauty with what would have passed among our ancestors as the middle stages of malnutrition. They go on perpetual diets, their minds taken up with calorie-counting, their bodies made feeble by hunger. "Dieting", says Wolf,

> is the most potent political sedative in women's history.... [C]oncern with weight leads to a virtual collapse of self-esteem and sense of effectiveness".[201]

---

[200] Rukshana Mosam, "Where Sex Adds Up", *Ms London*, London, 8th May 1989.

[201] Naomi Wolf, "The Beauty Myth", *The Sunday Times*, London, 9th September

It must be confronted and rejected. Control of advertising is one means to this end.

After the feminists come certain homosexuals who feel oppressed every time they see an advert showing a married couple. There is the ecological movement, opposing all advertising that promotes the use of non-renewable resources. There are various moral conservatives and national socialists, crying out against the promotion of allegedly immoral products or relationships.

So far, these groups have achieved nothing in the way of regulation. But it requires only a change of government for some of their views to become rather more important than they have been during the past twelve years of Conservative rule. Alternatively, like the health activists, they can look expectantly to Brussels.

iii: The European Community

I come now to the European Community, increasingly regarded as a *deus ex machina* by every group, liberal or collectivist, that cannot get its way at home. Except insofar as its members are directly influenced by the health activists or other campaigners, the European Commission is not opposed to advertising. Its chief end in this as in every other matter is the creation of a single market, the means to this being the harmonising of rules and standards. No member state must be more liberal than another, nor more restrictive. There must be a common protection of copyright and patents, common weights and measures, common levels of taxation. Everything, so far as possible, must be the same throughout the Community. Its controls, both actual and proposed, on advertising are a theoretical average of those already in force within the member states: each government must reduce or extend its controls until the common average is reached.

Where the weight of taxes on alcohol and tobacco is concerned, harmonisation will be for the British public a decidedly liberal measure. It will bring big reductions of prices. But for advertising, it will be restrictive. The governments of the other member states do

---

1990. Her book, from which this article is condensed, I have not yet read.

more to control advertising than our own currently does. They have been more heavily influenced by the various pressure groups. Therefore, to reach the theoretical common average, our own controls will need to be increased.

There are two European laws already in place. More have been proposed.

First, there is the Cross-Frontier Broadcasting Directive, adopted by the Council of Ministers in the October of 1989. This is to some extent a liberalising measure. It allows free transmission from any one member state throughout all the others. So long as broadcasting within that member state is governed by the Directive, no controls can be imposed on the reception of its transmissions for any reason but the protection of morals. It also allows comparative advertising—that is attacks on the quality goods or services of a rival supplier compared with one's own—this not currently being permitted in the British electronic media.

In all else, though, the Directive restricts British advertising. It limits the amount of time per day given by any broadcaster to advertising to no more than 15 per cent of total transmission time. It bans the advertising of all tobacco products, both direct and indirect. It bans the advertising of prescription medicines and treatments. It allows the advertising of alcohol, but only subject to the kind of restrictions described above.

Second, there is the Misleading Advertising Directive, adopted in 1984. This bans all advertising claims that are not strictly true. For example, another name must be given to Scotch eggs if they are not made in Scotland; and to French bread baked anywhere but in France. Prawn cocktail flavoured crisps cannot be sold if they are found to taste of something else.

There is a proposed Directive to ban false advertising claims about the quality and other characteristics of food; another to restrict the advertising of branded pharmaceuticals; another to ban the advertising of financial services.

Then, on the 15th of May, 1991, a proposed Draft Directive was agreed by the Commission, to ban the advertising and promotion of all tobacco products throughout the Community. An exception would be made for adverts placed inside tobacconists' shops. Otherwise, the ban would be total. No newspaper or magazine could go on sale if it carried adverts for tobacco products. Publications from outside the Community would also be banned if found to contain tobacco adverts. Mrs Vasso Papandreou, the Commissioner responsible for this proposal, announced that it would cover every kind of visual representation, "down to the overalls of Formula One drivers".[202]

This Draft Directive was successfully opposed by the British Government, claiming that its own voluntary system of regulation was already enough. We can be sure, however, that it will be proposed again. Of course, although strongly supported by the various Community health lobbies, it has less to do with the medical case against tobacco than with the alleged need for harmonisation. In France, Spain, Italy, Belgium and Portugal, tobacco advertising is banned. Therefore, the ban must be made common to the whole Community. If it were banned in only one member state, the Commission might well be pressing for liberalisation—as was the case recently in Greece, where the government was ordered to lift a ban on the advertising of children's toys.

Whatever it finally does with regard to the advertising of tobacco, the Community is not expected to alter the £650 million subsidy paid each year to tobacco farmers through the Common Agricultural Policy.[203] That is a wholly separate matter.

II: In Defence of Advertising

Though I mention them, as measures welcomed or indirectly prompted by the enemies of advertising, any full discussion of these Community regulations falls outside the scope of my current enquiry. Their immediate cause is the belief that harmonisation is most effectively achieved by administrative decree rather than free

---

[202] *The Daily Telegraph*, London, 16th May 1991.

[203] *Ibid.*

competition. I am inclined to doubt this. My own view is that the Community's best future lies as a union of sovereign states—extending far beyond its present twelve members—united by a common adherence to the ideals of free enterprise, democracy and the rule of law. On this view, there is no need for the vast flood of regulations now pouring out of Brussels. The Commission's only proper function is to resolve economic disputes between the member states, and to represent the Community in trade discussions with other nations or groups of nations. This, however, is part of the debate on federalism, and belongs to another pamphlet.

By all means, what I have to say concerning the regulation of advertising applies as much to Community regulation as to any other. But my real argument is with the health activists and similar groups. Their attack on advertising is purely an attack on freedom of speech. There is no distracting justification from them on the grounds of administrative convenience or relatively liberal harmonisation. For them, the attack on advertising is a direct and necessary attack on one of those core principles that have raised Western civilisation to its present ascendency, and which the provinces and satellite states of the former Soviet Empire are now struggling so hard to embrace.

i: Freedom of Speech

The case against censorship is simply put. While the public order may sometimes require controls on certain types of its expression, no opinion is ever to be suppressed. That opinion may be absurd. It may be grossly offensive. It may recommend the most dangerous or alarming things. But this is of no importance. Freedom of speech, for all its apparent disadvantages, is the means by which all other freedoms are protected. Take that away, or seriously abridge it, and all else may and will also be taken.

To give an extreme example, would the National Socialists have found it so easy to murder nine million non-combatant prisoners had the deportations and gassings been freely reported in the German media? Would the Hitler régime have lasted even beyond 1938 had its actions been known and openly discussed in Germany?

To give a milder example, our own country is by international standards a model of democracy and constitutional freedom. But its system of government is not without fault. The police are sometimes corrupt and partial, the courts sometimes idle or incompetent in the sifting of evidence. Wrong convictions are occasionally made, and the authorities have every interest in not confessing to their mistake. There are instances where public funds are wasted or embezzled; or where the whole weight of bureaucracy comes wrongly down onto the individual, and the law gives no easy redress. There is no malevolence at work in our system to compare with that of the old Soviet and South African systems. But we are ruled by human beings, and they would need to be saints if they never misused their power. What keeps them to the path of right and justice is the force of public opinion, directed and expressed by a vigilant free press. Muzzle that, and not all the democratic and legal machinery that human ingenuity can devise would be so effective on our behalf.

But this is a negative case, stressing the defence of what is already possessed. It is supplemented by the positive case—that to suppress an opinion is to place a check on the progress of humanity. There are two parts to this.

ii: Whether Correct

First, an opinion may be correct, and this in spite of all appearances to the contrary. I doubt if there is one person reading these words who has not in the past believed with utter certainty in something that later turned out to be a falsehood. The most casual knowledge of history gives instances of truths laughed at and their discoverers persecuted. Galileo when a feeble old man, going blind, was led round an Inquisition torture chamber, and had explained to him how its instruments would be used against him—unless he would "freely" retract the damnable heresy of asserting that the Earth was in orbit about the Sun. The German National Socialists drove physicists into exile or idleness for refusing to denounce the "Jewish" myth of the interchangeability of energy and matter. The Soviet Socialists were less considerate: they simply killed those biologists who denied the Lysenkoist claim, that acquired characteristics were transmissible to the next generation. Everyone knows how the Roman Church made itself a laughing stock well into the nineteenth century for its defence

157

of the Ptolemaic cosmology. The Germans lost the race to develop the first atom bomb. Soviet agriculture must have lost somewhat by the twenty year rejection of Mendelian genetics—though, set beside the losses brought by collectivisation and the mass-murder of peasants, it would be hard to assess any further losses even had salt been used for fertiliser. But this is to digress. So far as the truth is worth knowing—and it always is to someone—we lose by its suppression.

iii: Whether False

Second, even if shown to be wrong beyond all reasonable doubt, to suppress an opinion is to deprive us of what John Stuart Mill calls "almost as great a benefit, the clearer perception and livelier impression of truth, produced by its collision with error"[204]. Protect the most solidly based truth with penal laws, and faith in it will insensibly wither.

Take, for example, the case of Dr Immanuel Velikovsky. His most famous work, *Worlds in Collision*, published in 1950,[205] is part

---

[204] Mill, *On Liberty, op. cit.*, Chapter II, Of the Liberty of Thought and Discussion.

See also Macaulay. Though undoubtedly a snob as regards advertising, he was a firm liberal when it came to a defence of speech in general. He says:

> "Men are never so likely to settle a question as when they discuss it freely. A government can interfere in discussion only by making it less free than it would otherwise be. Men are most likely to form just opinions when they have no other wish than to know the truth, and are exempt from all influence, either of hope or fear. Government, as government, can bring nothing but the influence of hope and fears to support its doctrines. It carries on controversy, not with reasons, but with threats and bribes. If it employs reasons, it does so, not by virtue of any powers which belong to it as a government. Thus, instead of a contest argument and argument, we have a contest between argument and force. Instead of an argument in which truth, from the natural constitution of the human mind, has a decided advantage over falsehood, we have a contest in which truth can be victorious only by accident" (Review of Southey's Colloquies (1829), in *Essays, op. cit.*, Vol. 2, p. 209).

[205] Immanuel Velikovsky, *Worlds in Collision*, Macmillan, New York, 1950.

nonsense, part lies. It upholds the literal truth of the miracles described in the Old Testament by assuming a mass of astronomical disturbances. Some time around 1500 BC, a giant comet is supposed to have detached itself from Jupiter and come close to the Earth on two occasions before crashing into Venus. On its first encounter, it either stopped or slowed down the rotation of our planet for a while, so causing the parting of the Red Sea and the other unusual events recorded in the book of *Exodus*. On its second, it made the walls of Jericho fall down, and the Sun appear to stand still in the sky as requested by Joshua during his battle with the Amorites. Then, around 700 BC, Mars is supposed to have strayed from its orbit, coming close to the Earth just in time to destroy Sennacherib's army—though without harming the walls of Jerusalem—and fulfill sundry prophecies made by Amos, Isaiah and others.

How anyone could have read this with a straight face, let alone have believed any of it, defeats me. Yet the book was an international best-seller. Whether ignorant of science or destitute of common sense, many reviewers heaped the most lavish praise on it. John O'Neill, the science editor of *The New York Herald Tribune*, called it "a magnificent piece of scholarly research". Ted Thackrey, editor of *The New York Compass*, suggested that what Velikovsky had discovered might "well rank him in contemporary and future history with Galileo, Newton, Planck, Kepler, Darwin, Einstein...".[206]

The scientists were outraged. Many wrote to the publisher, threatening to boycott its scientific texts. Some of the writers of those texts threatened to write in future for other publishers. Eventually, the publication rights were turned over to another house, and the associate editor who had first realised the book's potential was sacked. The response to Velikovsky, said Eric Larabee, the editor of *Harper's* magazine, was a "disgrace to American science". He was shocked at the lack of faith shown by the scientists in the "open testing of ideas".[207]

---

[206] Quoted in Martin Gardner, *Fads and Fallacies in the Name of Science*, Dover Publications, New York, 1957, p. 31.

[207] Quoted in *ibid.*, p.323.

But here the persecution had to end. Its publishers could be punished: the book itself could not be suppressed, but had to be refuted point by point. For the next few years, it had to be pointed out—that planets are not known to wander in and out of their orbits; that even a gentle slowing of the Earth's rotation would have produced a universal catastrophe with effects still plainly to be seen.

Destroying Velikovsky's reputation may have been an annoyingly long task. It may have seemed a waste of time set against all the other exciting developments of the 1950s. Even so, it was more fruitful than suppression. No one who followed the controversy could fail to learn something of physics and astronomy. Many who had accepted what they had learned at school with a languid assent were now set thinking for themselves, and emerged with a firmer apprehension of the truth. The final effects of the controversy were beneficial to the progress of science. As Charles Darwin had written a century before,

> [f]alse facts are highly injurious to the progress of science, for they often endure long; but false views, if supported by some evidence, do little harm, for everyone takes a salutary pleasure in proving their falseness; and when this is done, one path toward error is closed and the road to truth is often at the same time opened.[208]

Suppose, however, the conventional physics and astronomy had been dogmas as firmly established in America as Lysenkoism then was throughout the Soviet Empire; suppose the more authoritarian scientists had been given their way, and Velikovsky's book had been withdrawn, and he forbidden to continue his research and to publish anything further—what then? Why, it would have been presumed by the great majority that the truth lay with him who was suffering. Little regard would have been given thereafter to views that, however plausibly presented, with whatever apparent weight of supporting evidence, could not stand alone, but had to be upheld by the coercive authority of the law. Everyone might have taken some interest in the Velikovsky thesis, passed on by word of mouth or in samizdat

---

[208] Quoted in *ibid.*, p.321.

editions: no one might so much as listened to the official refutations.

If, therefore, we desire the benefits of progress, we must leave opinions alone. We must leave people free to seek out and announce whatever they think to be truth of any matter. We must be like the gold-panners, who for the occasional quarter ounce of gold must wash endless tons of rubbish through their sieves. We must tolerate all the nonsense that comes off the printing press and over the airwaves—flat-earthism, creationism, socialism, protectionism, satanic child-abuse scares, and so on without limit. We must seek an answer to these not in censorship but in the greater, if often less rapid, power of unarmed truth.

iv: Whether Advertising Qualifies as Speech

The enemies of advertising seldom reply to these arguments. Instead, they dismiss them as not applying to the case in hand, or they give freedom of speech a definition all their own. Thus David Simpson, the former Director of ASH, once wrote to various newspapers, demanding that they should stop publishing replies to his own arguments. Describing these replies as "misrepresentations" and "quotations out of context", he asked that

> editors should seriously question whether it is really in their readers' interests even to publish the propaganda of the tobacco lobby.[209]

In an earlier letter, he had declared that

> [t]o publish letters from these wretched people is a somewhat perverted extension of the concept of free speech.[210]

---

[209] David Simpson,"Letter" *The Droitwich Advertiser*, 8th January 1987.

[210] Idem, "Letter", *The Doctor*, 24th July 1986. In the same issue, the Editor replied as follows:

> As a newspaper we respect all points of view, though not necessarily agreeing with them. If the time ever comes when we deny a reader the right to express a reasonable opinion merely because it opposes our own,

Since even the expression of views with which Mr Simpson disagrees is not allowed to pass as free speech, I can understand his unwillingness to consider any case for the right to advertise.

I turn, however, to the more respectable argument against regarding advertising as speech. It is claimed that some distinction exists ordinary and commercial speech, and that only the former ought to be protected. This strikes me as an odd distinction. Take the following: "My vitamin C injections are good for you"; "Jesus died for mankind"; "Political power, properly so called, is merely the organised power of one class for oppressing another". Though what they claim is different, these statements are of exactly the same type. Each makes a factual assertion, implicitly urging a certain course of action. Each can be supported or rejected by arguments of varying force. Suppressing any is an attack on the free communication of ideas. Professor Burt Newborne, former National Legal Director of the American Civil Liberties Union, agrees. He believes that

> [b]anning speech about lawful choices—whether economic or political—treats people like rats in a laboratory maze. Seeking to guide behaviour patterns that seem "wiser" to the elite and rationing the flow of public information, is an Orwellian process that has no place in our system of political and economic democracy.[211]

Yet a distinction is made. The most popular currently is based on motive. Preachers and politicians seek to persuade, we are told—advertisers only to make money. So Caspar Henderson, writing in the otherwise admirable *Index on Censorship*: "Before anything else advertisements are made to persuade people to buy things".[212] Therefore, whatever their apparent form, they cannot be speech. Bring in the profit motive, he seems to believe, and a

---

expect a hammer and sickle to be part of our banner.

[211] Quoted from his Commentary: "Censorship Stifles Choice", in *Phillip Morris Magazine*, May/June, 1990, p. 43.

[212] *Index on Censorship*, London vol. 20, no. 1 (January 1991), p. 4.

censorship that he might elsewhere condemn, becomes justifiable regulation.

v: J.S. Mill's Ambiguity

This is a principle that appears to have been accepted by Mill. His distinction between "self-regarding" and "other-regarding" acts—a distinction seized on by every one of his critics, from James Fitzjames Stephen all the way down to Mary Whitehouse—lets him proceed to the conclusion that

> ...trade is a social act. Whoever undertakes to sell any description of goods to the public, does what affects the interest of other persons, and of society in general; and thus his conduct, in principle, comes within the jurisdiction of society.... [T]he... doctrine of Free Trade... rests on grounds different from, though equally solid with, the principle of individual liberty asserted in this Essay.[213]

This in turn lets him flirt with socialism without having to admit its incompatibility with freedom in the liberal sense. The flirtation, though, is not wholly safe, for it leaves his doctrine of absolute freedom of speech open to attack. If I incite or procure you to commit a murder, I can be punished as a principal to the act. There is no difficulty here, and Mill admits none. But suppose I persuade you to drink yourself into alcoholism. You ought not to be punished, for you are harming only yourself. Ought I to be punished, for having advised you to harm yourself? No, he says, for that is a self-regarding act:

> If people must be allowed, in whatever concerns only themselves, to act as seems best to themselves, at their own peril, they must equally be free to consult with one another about what is fit to be so done; to exchange opinions, and give and receive suggestions. Whatever it is permitted to do, it must be permitted to advise to do.[214]

---

[213] Mill, *On Liberty, op, cit.,* p. 150 (Chapter V, "Applications").

[214] *Ibid.,* p.154.

But suppose I am a publican, or have some other financial interest in the sale of alcoholic beverages—does this defence cover advertising? That is an activity intimately connected with trade, and "trade is a social act". Mill continues, with evident perplexity:

> The question is doubtful only when the instigator derives a personal benefit from his advice; when he makes it his occupation, for subsistence or pecuniary gain, to promote what society and the State consider to be an evil. Then, indeed, a new element of complication is introduced; namely, the existence of classes of persons with an interest opposed to what is considered as the public weal and whose mode of living is grounded on the conteraction of it. Ought this to be interfered with, or not?[215]

He devotes a page and a half to equivocation, giving no clear answer is. He plainly hates the thought on any limitation on his arguments for freedom of speech, but also wants to leave the way open to some public control of economic activity. But, whatever Mill may have thought of advertising, his chosen distinction between acts has allowed a potential distinction between kinds of speech that can be exploited by anyone who cares to read him.[216]

vi: The American Courts

The principle has also been accepted, if only partially, by the American courts. Speech is protected by the First Amendment to the Constitution of the United States:

> Congress shall make no law respecting an establishment of

---

[215] *Ibid.*

[216] The reader will, of course, realise that Mill's confusion over acts is logically distinct from his arguments regarding speech, which stand or fall by themselves. As a liberal conservative, I venerate Mill as a great man. But unlike the adherents of the totalitarian ideologies must their intellectual leaders, I am not compelled to regard our intellectual leaders with slavish adoration. For the parts of it that are true, *On Liberty* is among the noblest works ever written. Other parts of it are very sad stuff, and no good purpose is served by denying this.

religion, or prohibiting the free exercise thereof; or abridging the freedom of speech, or of the press; or the right of the people peaceably to assemble, and to petition the Government for a redress of grievances.

A liberal construction has allowed the widest freedom of expression. Publications that here would pass furtively from hand to hand are openly sold in America. But commercial speech lies partly outside this protection. In a recent case, for example, the Federal Trade Commission prosecuted the R.J. Reynolds Tobacco Co. Inc. for having run a false and misleading advert in the press. The Company had disputed certain claims made about the connection between smoking and heart disease. The Company won—but only because its advert had not mentioned any prices or brand names. As such, it constituted "speech", and was held to be exempt from regulation no matter how false. But the mention of a price or brand name might, all else remaining unchanged, have degraded it to a common advert, fit for regulation in the public interest.[217]

vii: No Reasonable Distinction

Nevertheless, this distinction, between ordinary and commercial speech, is at best groundless. It follows from the premise, that love of money is a more wicked motive for lying than any other. It lets me lie my head off to get people into church or a trade union. I can talk about my conversations with God, or how splendidly the workers live in some distant country where no foreign journalists are allowed.

---

[217] See Douglass J. Den Uyl & Tibor R. Machan, "Should Cigarette Advertising be Banned?", in *Public Affairs Quarterly*, 2 (4), October 1988, pp. 19-30.

To what extent it might have been degraded remains ambiguous. The Supreme Court has held commercial speech to be protected by the First Amendment, but not to the same extent as non-commercial speech. It is said that total bans on truthful commercial advertising conveying information of value to a diverse audience are now untenable in the United States, although the precise limits of government regulation are still being cautiously redefined. (J.J. Boddewyn, "Tobacco Advertising in a Free Society", in Robert D. Tollison (ed), *Smoking and Society: Toward a More Balanced Assessment*, D.C. Heath and Company, Lexington, Mass., 1986, p. 320).

All this is speech. I have a right to say it. Anyone who tries to silence me will earn—and deserve—the full blast of liberal outrage. But let me just hint that my vitamin C injections—only £19.99 each—will make people better in bed, and the cry will go up for action against me, with scarcely a word said in my favour. That is not speech, but vulgar advertising.

Yet a motive is good or bad only in proportion to its likely effects. I have no doubt that certain companies do rather well from the promotion of dangerous or disagreeable lifestyles. But, unless we are to regard profit as an absolute evil, every attack on advertising, made on the grounds described, applies vastly more to the advocates of Christianity and Communism. Jesus may well have died for us. To be sure, millions, and perhaps tens of millions, have been killed in his name. The Marxists have tried repeatedly since 1917 to build a road to their classless utopia. Every time, that road has led nowhere. Every time, it has been paved with corpses. I am not arguing for the suppression of the *Bible* or the works of Karl Marx. But, if we are to distinguish statements according to the motives behind their utterance, why ever pick on advertising? We might as reasonably run about turning off the bath taps on a sinking ship.

viii: No Unique Pecuniary Motive to Advertising

Of course, it may be that I have missed the point—that pecuniary motives are uniquely impure regardless of their consequences. But, assuming this were true, it could only be used against advertising by those of its enemies who give their time to the battle free of charge. The feminists and others who go about denouncing advertising as intellectual prostitution may deserve to be answered directly. Many of the health activists, though, who sneer at paid advocacy ought first to explain their own motives. For, "[t]he anti-smoking movement" says Peter L. Berger,

> is no longer a little band of lonely zealots. Rather, the movement is large, well organized, and providing employment as well as status to sizeable numbers of people.... [It] is most strongly represented among the most educated segments of the upper middle class (segments sometimes designated as the

New Class or the knowledge class—broadly speaking, the intelligentsia). This stratum has a collective interest in government as against the private sector because, compared with other segments of the middle class, it derives more of its income and status from government expenditures and government programs.[218]

Perhaps these salaried employees are passionately committed to the truth of what they are hired to propagate. But that still does not distinguish them from the copy writer who believes that Brand X really is a wonderful cigarette. It is dishonesty or stupidity to claim otherwise.

ix: A Practical Case for Admitting Some Advertising as Speech

However, so far as the health activist case is concerned, the best argument for free advertising is practical. That case has not been fully made out. We are being urged into a potentially dangerous course of restriction on the basis of an hypothesis that has yet to be demonstrated.

The health activist claims derive mostly from epidemiological research. Now, whatever its value in the past, epidemiology today is a largely redundant science. It is best suited to tracing the causes of an infectious disease. Antibiotics have brought these under control. During the last two generations, there has been a shortage of diseases in which its methods are likely to produce good results. In consequence, the epidemiologists have turned increasingly to the tracing of associations between the main degenerative illnesses—such as heart disease and the various cancers—and specific habits of personal characteristics.

The problem here is that it is impossible to derive causal connections from associations. There are too many variable causes, both known and unknown, for any certain conclusions to be reached. When a new diseases is traced to its proper cause—by the appropriate laboratory

---

[218] Peter L. Berger, "Environmental Tobacco Smoke: Ideological Issue and Cultural Issue", in Robert D. Tollison (ed), *Clearing the Air: Perspectives on Environmental Tobacco Smoke*, D.C. Heath, Lexington, Mass.,1988, pp. 85-86.

research—the epidemiologists are generally found to have been wrong. For example, when the first cases of AIDS appeared in California, the epidemiologists applied all their usual methods to finding a cause. They looked at ethnic and religious background, at the amounts of alcohol and tobacco and other drugs consumed by the victims, at residential and occupational histories, at sexual habits. They found a strong association with the use of amyl nitrate, and suggested this as the cause of the disease. The association was very strong—as strong as that between cigarette smoking and lung cancer. As we know, AIDS is not caused by the use of amyl nitrate.[219]

When associations are turned into causal connections, one can usually find ignorance or dishonesty at work.

Look at the claims made regarding nutrition. According to the Report cited above,

> The higher the level of cholesterol in the blood the greater the risk of heart disease....

> There is good evidence that the amount of saturated fat (derived mostly from animal fats) in the diet is an important determinant of cholesterol levels.[220]

According to Dr James Le Fanu, "this thesis is plausible, but it leaks like a colander".[221] The epidemiological research on which it is based is defective, he says. He refers to the famous cross-cultural study begun by Ancel Keys, in which the incidence of heart disease in various countries was correlated with the consumption of dairy

[219] See J.P. Vandenbroucke & V.P.A.M. Pardoel, "An Autopsy of Epidemiological Methods: The Case of 'Poppers' in the Early Epidemic of the Human Immuniodeficiency Syndrome (AIDS)", *American Journal of Epidemiology*, 1989, 129, pp. 455-57.

[220] Smith & Jacobson, *op. cit.*, p. 31.

[221] James Le Fanu, "Diet and Disease: Nonsense and Non-science", Digby Anderson (ed), *A Diet of Reason: Sense and Nonsense in the Healthy Eating Debate*, The Social Affairs Unit, London, 1986, p. 119.

produce. It was apparently shown how Japanese immigrants to America who adopted the high-fat diet of their new country also acquired a higher risk of heart disease. But it seems that no such correlation was shown where two similar countries were compared, nor when different groups of people within the same country were compared. Nor did the subsequent laboratory research ever show how fat consumption was causally related to cholesterol levels.

Le Fanu concludes that there is no proven link between the amount of fat eaten and the incidence of heart disease. The link is made in order to encourage us to the adoption of a diet that owes more to the cultural ideology of the nutritionists than to their scientific research. He condemns the various committees that make it their business to tell us otherwise:

> In all their self-righteous admonitions to the public they appear blind to the serious consequences of their propaganda, that it misinforms the public about the complexity of disease, trivialises tragedy, blames patients for their illnesses, stigmatises the dairy industry and degrades medicine as a science-based profession.[222]

I am not saying that Le Fanu is right and the authors of the Report wrong. I am not qualified to judge. All I can tell is that Le Fanu is respected as a medical writer and an expert on heart disease. If he is willing so flatly to deny that animal fats are necessarily bad for the heart, I must doubt the assumption made in the Report, that this particular debate is now closed.

Look also at the claims made regarding tobacco. Many of these are at least exaggerated. So far as can be told, smokers do face a higher than average risk of lung cancer and heart disease. We can argue over the reasons why. But the evidence itself appears as certain as such evidence can be. Nevertheless, many other claims handed down to us as demonstrated truths appear to rest on nothing more than assertion. For the most alarming claim, that smokers can cause fatal illnesses in the non-smokers around them, there is no good evidence. Every so

---

[222] *Ibid.*, p.124.

often, the world is presented with yet another "conclusive study". Those published over the past generation have varied between the ambiguous and the dishonest. Having reviewed about a hundred of them, Peter N. Lee reports so many persistent misclassifications as to account for all the alleged associations between passive smoking and lung cancer. Its meaning plainly spelled out, none of the studies, he believes, has so far given anyone with so much as a trace of common sense the smallest grounds for worry.[223]

Uncertainty, I grant, is not in itself sufficient reason for not taking action. If it were, nothing would ever be done, good or bad. But we are dealing here with a set of claims that affect our very lives. We have the strongest reason possible for wanting to know the truth. That truth may have been discovered already by the health activists. But has not yet been finally established. In the meantime, it must be tested and refined by the fullest and most free public discussion. The people most likely to make or finance the opposing case are the manufacturers concerned. It might be desirable on this account if they were to confine themselves, like the R.J. Reynolds Tobacco Company, to the pure conveying of information, without the mentioning of brand names or prices or the use of the normal selling techniques. But human nature being what it is, some financial interest will need to be gratified if the case is to be made. Therefore, advertising must be not merely permitted, but encouraged—and all

---

[223] Peter N. Lee, *Misclassification of Smoking Habits and Passive Smoking: A Review of the Evidence*, Springer-Verlag, Berlin, 1988.

The current fashion is to refer sceptics to the *Fourth Report of the Independent Scientific Committee on Smoking and Health*, a 68 page document published by the Government in the March of 1988. This Report does, indeed, support the claim, that a non-smoking spouse of a smoker runs somewhere between a 10 per cent and 30 per cent greater risk of contracting lung cancer than the non-smoking spouse of a non-smoker. But, if we look to this support, rather than what is most often piled on it, we see that the risk of lung cancer is estimated to rise from 10:100,000 to 12 or 13:100,000. In the first place, only a fool or a fanatic without regard for common sense could panic at a risk so trivial. In the second, a statistical variation so wide may be taken as pretty meaningless (See T.E. Utley, "Morality Overcome by Fumes", *The Times*, London, 29th March 1988).

for the sake of our health.

Moreover, even granting that the current health orthodoxy were the proven truth, the advertising of unhealthy products or lifestyles would still be justified. Look at cigarette advertising. In an age where most smokers have paid some attention to the health warnings, they are predisposed to change to whatever brand can reasonably be claimed as safer. Thus, they will increasingly buy cigarettes with filters or better filters, and with lower stated tar contents. Where tobacco advertising is banned, these changes are delayed. It was banned in Norway in 1975. Filter sales there in 1982 accounted for 85 per cent of the cigarette market. In this country, where advertising is only regulated, they accounted for 94 per cent of the market.[224] Clearly, in this case, an advertising ban has prevented the free flow of information. It is no different from any other act of censorship. So far as knowledge about filter tips and low tar contents save lives, it is a worse act than many others.

x: Adverts Allow Other Forms of Speech

Finally, advertising, whatever its status as specch, whatever its effect on the health debate, is necessary for the maintenance of a free press. Its value to the British press was estimated in 1988 at £6,961 million.[225] This is a lot of money; but even its small diminution would be keenly felt. The quality dailies drew nearly 65 per cent of their total revenue from the sale of advertising space; the quality Sundays nearly 30 per cent. The loss of tobacco advertising alone—never mind alcohol, pharmaceuticals and financial services—would bring revenue losses of 0.26 per cent and 4.29 per cent respectively. Perhaps these are small losses. But, for an industry where profit margins are low, or even negative, they can still be expected to have a significant effect on profitability. Some papers might close. Others might reduce their coverage. There would be fewer articles of first

---

[224] Boddewyn, *op. cit.*, p. 315

[225] I obtained these figures, and those following, from the Advertising Association.

rate quality, and fewer reviews of the arts and sciences. Since the popular papers earn more of their revenue from sales to the public, and tend to have higher profit margins, they would be less affected. The net effect, therefore, of a ban only on tobacco advertising would be to take the British press on the whole still further down market. The relative influence of the tabloid press on opinion—already widely condemned within the educated classes—would be increased.

xi: Other Defences

Nor is it only on the grounds of freedom of speech that advertising can be defended. There are other grounds. Consider:

Wider Consequences of Censorship

First, the enemies of advertising are often the enemies of all freedom. The ideology of the health lobby, for example, is a kind of national socialism. The authors of the Report cited above

> believe that the health of its citizens is one of the most important resources needed by a nation for the pursuit of most other legitimate national objectives.[226]

Our bodies, on this reasoning, belong not to ourselves, but to the State. The very wording throughout much of the Report carries the reader back to Germany in the 1930s.[227] The only difference is that, then, the health lobby had no need for discretion. They openly attacked as a "liberal perversion" the view that one should have the right to dispose of his body as he saw fit—the *Recht auf den eigenen*

---

[226] Smith and Jacobson, *op. cit.*, p. 4.

[227] Take the quotation at the head of Chapter 8 (p. 105): "Medicine is a social science, & politics nothing but medicine on a grand scale". The author of this, Rudolph Virchow, died before Hitler came to power. But he was one of those theorists of medical authoritarianism who prepared the way for Joseph Mengele and all the other doctors who took it as their duty to help purge the *Volk* of undesirable elements. For a full discussion of the intimate connection between German medical opinion and national socialism, see Robert Proctor, cited below.

Körper. They spoke instead of the "obligation to be healthy"—the *Pflicht zur Gesundheit.*[228] Since health was now an integral part of the German national interest, they argued, it could no longer be possible to tolerate substances damaging to society as a whole, whatever the wishes of those individuals consuming them.[229]

For these people, controls on advertising are no more than a prelude to controls on the availability of products. There is no doubt that they want to ban smoking. For the authors of the Report,

> [t]he ultimate public health objective for cigarette smoking can be seen as the elimination of all but occasional cigarette smoking.[230]

According to Nigel Smith, "if tobacco was discovered tomorrow it would be banned".[231] It is allowed only because it is too familiar for people to see it as it is. His task is to strip away the veil of antiquity, after which the appropriate action can be taken.

David Simpson is still more emphatic. Speaking in 1990 on television, he declared that

> if cigarettes were invented today, there's no way they'd be allowed to be made, never mind advertised or promoted in any other way.... No decent society would actually allow, willy nilly, the promotion of a product even a tenth as dangerous as cigarettes. So that's why we want to ban them.[232]

---

[228] From Robert Proctor, *Racial Hygeine: Medicine under the Nazis*, Harvard University Press, Cambridge, Mass., 1988, p. 248.

[229] *Ibid*, p. 240.

[230] Smith & Jacobson, *op. cit.*, p. 77.

[231] BSB, *op. cit.*.

[232] "Right to Reply", Channel Four, 17th February, 1990. While quoting from statements made on television, I might as well add the words of Ms Joyce Epstein, the Assistant Director of ASH. Asked on the BBC programme, "Over

It may be unfair to put a literal meaning on words spoken unscripted in a television studio. Mr Simpson may have intended "ban" to govern not "cigarettes" but "advertised" and "promoted". Until he clarifies them, though, I will give his words their natural meaning. He is a prohibitionist.

We may disapprove of the advertising of products that are dangerous. But unless we also want the banning of the actual products, we must regard the calls for advertising bans as the thin end of a wedge.

Overestimated Power of Advertising

Second, there is no evidence that advertising bans achieve their desired end, of reducing consumption. The claims of the advertising industry have been taken at face value. Advertising is seen as an immensely powerful force for moulding opinion. Given the right approach and enough money, the belief seems to be, and Saatchi and Saatchi could create a market out of nothing for sugared cat mess. If only the advertisers could be silenced, the conclusion is, the market in unhealthy products would collapse.

This is an inflated view of advertising. It cannot create markets out of nothing. It cannot sustain them in decline. The history of advertising is littered with failed campaigns. 30 years ago, a new brand of cigarette, called Strand, was introduced. No amount of money could find it a place in the market. It was withdrawn. A few years earlier, in America, the Ford Motor Corporation had brought out the Edsel. Record sums were spent on its promotion. Again, it failed and was withdrawn. Think of quadrophonic gramophone records. Think of the Betamax format in this country. Think of moistened lavatory paper. Think of all the advertising money spent in vain to bolster the

---

to You", on the 12th August, 1989, whether cigarette should be banned completely, she answered that there was "no right to smoke". This is, of course, ambiguous. She might have been saying, that we have no right to do what she considers bad for us. Alternatively, she might have been giving voice to the dreadful—and perfectly un-English—notion, that whatever is not specifically allowed by the law is forbidden. In either case, I scarcely need say, she would be hard put to raise any principled objection to Stalin or Hitler.

shrinking markets for Guiness and The Sun.

Neither can advertising bans can send a market into decline. Cigarette consumption has remained fairly constant in Norway since the 1975 advertising ban. Here, it has fallen by a quarter.[233] As for the effect on alcohol consumption, the advertising of whisky was banned in France in 1955. In that year, 157,000 proof gallons of whisky were imported. In 1979, 6,294,000 proof gallons were imported.[234]

The real purpose of most advertising is far more modest. It can establish or increase a supplier's share in a market that already exists. This is plainly the intention of drink and cigarette advertising. The companies are not seeking to enlarge the total market. Instead, each is competing for a larger share of a market that is in most wealthy countries either stationary or in decline.

The Economic Value of Advertising

Third, if advertising has any wider function, it is to maintain the efficient working of a market economy. Here, I feel that I ought briefly to digress and review the case for markets. The basic fact of life is scarcity. We have infinite wants, but only limited resources. We must allocate these resources to produce the greatest possible return of consumer satisfaction. If we make so many pencils, we can only make so many television sets. If we devote so much effort to producing consumer goods, we can only devote so much to producing capital equipment. Going back to the pencils, how do we get the greatest use out of them for the minimum outlay of effort? Do we use cheaper graphite that wears out quickly, or harder wearing but more expensive graphite? Do we secure the rubbers to the ends with plastic, to make which requires oil, or with brass, that may have to be brought from the other side of the world? What abrasive do we mix in with the rubber—silver sand or pumice stone? These are important questions. Answer any of them wrong, and we must have

---

[233] Boddewyn, *op. cit,.* pp. 315-6.

[234] Charles Plouviez, "Food Advertising Not the Problem", Anderson *op. cit.* 1986, p. 127.

fewer pencils or fewer televison sets.

The market economy tends to find the right answers. It does so because everything has a price that reflects its relative value. The entirety of human knowledge about cost is encoded in a vast structure of prices that reflects the subjective valuations of all economic goods at any one moment. The function of this structure is to express information in the briefest possible way about what goods are wanted, in what quantities, at what qualities, and by what means. These signals are responded to, or anticipated, by businessmen. The function of profit and loss is to show who is responding best.

I have just mentioned oil. Let us consider some of the effects of an increased demand for petrol. The first and most obvious will be a shortage at the pumps as the retailers sell out at the existing price. Next, faced with larger orders, the oil companies will put up their prices. Perhaps the supply of crude oil is fixed. More likely, it will cost more to bring further supplies to the market. In either case, prices will go up.

Now, oil is also used by the makers of paint and records, among many others. Faced with a rise in the cost of their main raw material, do these put up their prices or look for substitutes for oil? That depends on the technical options open to them and on the subjective valuations of their products. The paint makers might find stable or increasing demand in spite of higher prices. The record makers, on the other hand, might find it necessary to economise on oil. This in turn might lead the makers of substitutes to expand their activities, putting up the wages of their skilled workers, and improving business among the local estate agents by their sudden need for larger premises.

And it may persuade the pencil makers to switch from plastic to brass.

The responses to a single change in demand would continue throughout the entire economy, inducing further changes, great or small, without limit. To trace these responses years after the event, when all the information has been gathered to the centre, would perplex the cleverest statistician. To trace them at the time would be impossible. No one but a fool would ever try to predict them. Yet the encoding of information in prices allows every adjustment to be made—sometimes immediately, sometimes with a slight delay—and nearly always made by people who never understand the true need for making them.

Even in a state of pure equilibrium, a central planning authority would never be able to gather the smallest fraction of what is passed on by the price mechanism, let alone respond to it. In the real world, where the pattern of choices shifts from moment to moment, any attempt to do without the market must result in chaos. It must result in an orgy of waste. When no one knows what is relatively scarce, everything will be squandered in reckless profusion until it runs out. No one, very likely, will even what to buy the few goods that eventually get produced.

It is the general function of advertising to help in the co-ordination of economic activity. It is by advertising in all its forms that knowledge is made generally available to both producers and consumers. Without it, competition would suffer. Without that, we should suffer.

Entrenchment of Oligopoly

Fourth, and following on from the above, the tendency of advertising bans is often to preserve established firms from the competition of new entrants to a market. The tobacco companies claim to be alarmed at the prospect of not being able to advertise. Perhaps they are for the moment. But let them quietly agree among themselves how much market share each should have, and they would join in the call for a ban. That would freeze all effective competition. They would be unable to attract each other's customers away. But they would also be secured from the risk of having their customers attracted away by any new entrant to the market. The various professional bodies made this discovery more than a century ago, and their members have benefitted ever since.

Intolerance as Folly of the Weak

Fifth, I sympathise with those minority groups which object to the ideological content of advertising. This does undoubtedly exist. The feminists and other radical "deconstructionists" are partly right: advertising does often go beyond the simple promotion of a product, to the promotion of whole lifestyles or ideologies. Recall a typical advert: A father and his young son come back filthy from some manly sport into a large and spotlessly clean kitchen. Does his wife throw a fit? Does she go upstairs and swallow a handful of valium? No, she smiles and waves a box of washing powder. Soon, the clothes are clean, ready to be soiled again. We have here the portrayal of enough sexual and economic stereotypes to have the average sociologist foaming at the mouth. The message is that women must be endlessly active and subservient to their menfolk; that a man must earn the sort of living that will let him afford a big house and a wife to run it for him; that boys must be toughened so that they too can survive in the marketplace when grown up. There is no hint of sexual non-conformity. Everyone is white. The parents are both about 35. If there is another child, it is a younger daughter, who stays by her mother and even helps with the housework.

The same method can be applied to almost any other advert. I remember one where a ruggedly handsome individualist could get service at a crowded bar simply by muttering "Cinzano"; another where a man, by smoking St Bruno in his pipe, became so attractive to women that he needed guards to keep them away; another where two barristers walk through the Law Courts, arguing whether or not the scantily dressed young woman ahead of them has used Silvikrin hair spray.

All this, I am certain, is deeply insulting to some people. But anyone who thinks it supremely powerful is showing no sense of proportion. Whoever claims that every man who enjoys the Flake advert is also learning that women like to be raped is a fool of the Millie Tant variety.

I might also add that no unpopular minority, unless it is also the governing elite, can afford to advocate censorship. It is a weapon that can be forged by anyone, but is used most often by the strong. Look again at the latest voluntary agreement with the tobacco companies. It was agreed that no cigarette advertisements should appear in any magazine with a female readership of more than 200,000, of whom a third of more were aged between 15 and 24.

What is this but a gross insult to women? Do they need special protection of this kind? Girls of 15 may need protection—as may boys. But a woman of 18 is an adult. She has the vote. She can go into business on her own account. She can take on a mortgage. She can marry and divorce. She can be made bankrupt and be sent to prison. Had the men who drafted and signed this agreement forgotten these things? Or did they simply feel that, whatever changes of legal status have occurred during this century, they were still dealing with "little women"—inferior beings who ought to feel grateful for a firm, paternalist pat on the head? Or is it just another proof, to add to all the others, that power is used by the powerful?

III: Conclusion

I say, then, that advertising is a right that we allow to be breached only at our peril. It may be vulgar. It may tell lies. It may promote the wrong kind of views or lifestyles. But there are no means, logical or practical, by which it can be restricted except at costs that I regard as wholly unacceptable.

It will be said against me, I have no doubt, that I am simply arguing for the right of people who are already very wealthy to go on making money from the needless suffering of others—that I am using the great names and arguments of liberalism to defend the most sordid of motives. That, however, is an occupational hazard. Unless its enemies are able to mount a frontal assault, freedom of any kind is invariably attacked in its outermost extensions, in those places where it is often least convenient or productive of honour to fight in its defence. But it is there that the battle is won or lost. The ground is less stony and the banners flutter more bravely in the wind elsewhere on the field. But those who sit round their camp fires, boasting of how they will rout any attack on the right of the Conservative or Labour Parties to put their message across in *The Guardian* and *The Daily Telegraph*—they are simply announcing their intention to fight in some pathetic last stand, in which the battle will have been already lost, and in which they will be best advised for their own reputation with the victors to bury their useless weapons and creep out of sight.

I will defend the right to advertise no matter what is said against me, whether by friend or foe. I leave it to the reader to decide for his or herself whether I am sincere and whether the names and arguments used have been misused.

5. SAVING THE KIDDIES,
ENSLAVING ADULTS

I am going on BBC Radio Scotland this coming Sunday morning [27th October 2002] to discuss passive smoking and children. Some researcher at the Royal Brompton Hospital in London is claiming that children whose parents smoke at home have a higher than average chance of contracting a range of serious illnesses. According to the news release helpfully provided by the BBC researchers, the illnesses include asthma, meningitis, cot death, and something called "glue ear". I shall have only nine minutes in which to argue my case—nine minutes that I must share with at least two different groups of health fascists. I will therefore say here what I shall say only in part to the listeners.

The first point I will make is that the evidence on passive smoking of all kinds has not so far been convincing. It has been gathered by comparing the incidence of lung cancer and other diseases among non-smoking partners of non-smokers with that among non-smoking partners of smokers. Inevitably, such evidence is of poor quality. It relies heavily on answers to questionnaires. People forget and people lie. There has also—at least in the more famous studies—been a lack of rigorous control for other variables. In the Hirayama study of the 1980s, for example, there was no account taken of differential exposure to traffic pollution, or to pollution arising in the home from the use of solid fuels for heating and cooking. The British Department of Health has tried to minimise the effect of such errors by using meta-analysis. This is effectively taking a number of studies and averaging their results. Obviously, though, an average result is only as reliable as the initial results used to calculate it.

In any event, the average results are statistically insignificant. One claim, much used in the late 1980s, was that passive smoking increased a person's chance of contracting lung cancer by 30 per cent. The numbers on which this claim was based were far less dramatic. It was alleged that without exposure to other people's tobacco smoke, a person's chance of contracting lung cancer in any one year was one in ten thousand, and with exposure one in thirteen thousand. Even if this were not accounted for by statistical error, no one would pay sixpence to insure against such a risk. So much for that terrifying 30 per cent!

I have no great learning in epidemiology. But what little I have convinces me that no epidemiological claim of any kind—and certainly none regarding a connection between tobacco and ill health—is worth considering unless accompanied by full disclosure of the studies on which it is based. How many people were observed? When, where and for how long were they observed? If not directly observed, what checks were made on the accuracy of their answers to questioning? What investigations were made into other possible causes of the problem being studied? Whenever I have taken the trouble to look at the detailed studies, the claims have in all cases fallen apart. There have been other studies during the past decade, I grant, and I have not paid much attention to them. But I have no reason to suppose them any more rigorous in their methodology than those I looked at in the past. And I am sure that if a more certain connection had been found, it would have been made front page news everywhere in the world.

The second point I will make is less technical. Let us suppose for the sake of argument that the claims about child health were reasonably true. What would follow from this? The news release is silent on action, and I suppose I shall be told in the studio that parents must be exhorted—at their own expense as taxpayers—not to smoke at home when their children are about. But supposing they pay too little attention to these exhortations—as they doubtless will—what then? The natural answer is not that those using this research will sadly shake their heads and go away to other business. It is that if parents will not change their ways voluntarily, they must be compelled to change; and if this is not possible, their children must be removed to some place of alleged greater safety. Though I presently forget where, I have read claims that smoking near children constitutes "child abuse".

Now, I will ignore the facts of the enormous child welfare

bureaucracy that has grown up in this country—a bureaucracy that continually enlarges itself by discovering more excuses to steal children away. I will also ignore the documented facts of just how safe the places are to which children are normally stolen. What I will develop is the principle that I can see being established. If smoking at home is used as an excuse for intervention by the child welfare authorities, the principle is stated that interventions may be made whenever some aspect of home lifestyle can be connected with some danger to a child's health. This principle granted, however, it can be indefinitely extended.

Suppose—and I am inclined to think this likely—it could be shown that Asian children were put in above average danger in later life of haemorrhoids and stomach cancer by eating the spicy food given them by their parents. If we allow intervention in the case of parents who smoke, why not in the case of parents who use lots of curry powder or monosodium glutamate? Again, Jews are generally believed to have an above average chance of being depressed. Perhaps this is the result of some genetic difference. But it may also be an effect of the pressures to achieve put on Jewish children from a very young age. Again, many working classes appear to feed their children a diet of fish fingers and microchips. Perhaps these cause problems later in life.

Where should we draw the line? At present, on the whole, it is still drawn defensibly. If parents are causing some deliberate or recklessly negligent harm to their children, and this harm is great enough to be reasonably apparent, there is a case for intervention—but not otherwise. The main abuse by the authorities is still a matter of fabricated claims about things like "satanic abuse" or a minute dwelling on real neglect at home combined with a refusal to acknowledge possibly greater harm in the places of alleged safety. But let the principle stated above be accepted in the case of smoking, and no family in the country will be safe.

The truth, I suspect, is that most health fascists are not actually worried about children. Their real concern is to stop adults from smoking. When they started their war on tobacco in the 1960s, they were openly authoritarian in their assertion of the right to act as our guardians. Since then, they have been put on the defensive by the reply that adults should have the right to do with themselves as they please. Therefore, starting in the 1980s, they began to manufacture statistics about passive smoking. This allowed them to claim that smoking was not a purely self-regarding act, and so could be regulated in public to prevent harm to others.

Of course, the most important others to be protected are children. What we are seeing now is a use of what my friend Stuart Goldsmith calls the "saving the kiddies argument". This is used as an excuse to regulate adult behaviour when all other excuses have been found wanting. We see it used in arguments over Internet pornography, over general advertising, over drugs, and over just about everything that some adults may like to do but that others would like them not to do, and where an open justification for control has been rejected or cannot easily be imagined.

I do not accept any claim that I have so far seen that there is such a thing as passive smoking. But if it does exist, it is reasonable to suppose that children are among its unwilling victims. But the only response in a free society is to pay no legal attention. The world is an imperfect place, and no amount of lawmaking will make it perfect. Criminal laws are useful to help reduce the grosser harms we may be inclined to do each other. Civil law can reduce some of the more refined harms. But when laws are made to protect children from more than the most unreasonable acts or lifestyle choices of their parents, that is an abuse of law. Such laws are unlikely to produce their stated end. They are likely, indeed, to produce greater evils than those alleged in support of their making.

If I get to say all this on Sunday morning, I shall be surprised. But at least I have written it.

INDEX

P

Paris, 35, 47
Pepys, Samuel, 43
Peter the Great, Czar, 69
Petition of Right, 126
Pleasure, 94, 97
Pliny the Elder, 32, 33
Pollock, David, 151
Portugal, 35, 36, 38, 139, 155
Powell, J. Enoch, 137
Private Eye, 146
Procopius of Caesarea, 105
Proctor, Robert, 29, 172, 173
Protection of Children (Tobacco)
    Act 1986, 131

R

R.J. Reynolds Tobacco Company,
    170
Raleigh, Sir Walter, 36, 56, 64
Rand, Ayn, 85, 86, 87
Robinson, Kenneth, 113
Rochefort, Jorévin de, 43
Roman Church, vi, 60, 105, 157
Roman Empire, 57, 80, 82, 94
Rome, 36, 52, 93
Roscelin, 86
Royal College of Physicians, 83,
    103, 151
Russell, M.A.H., 23, 78, 98, 100,
    120, 121
Russia, 59, 69, 93

S

Saatchi brothers, 146
Salvius of Albi, 105, 106
Scotland, 65, 154, 181
Senior Service, 27
Sheridan, Richard Brinsley, 145
Simpson, David, 25, 30, 57, 75,

119, 161, 162, 173, 174
Sin, 94, 108
Skoal Bandit, 27
Social Affairs Unit, The, 147,
    168
Socialism, 28
Southey, Robert, 158
Spain, 31, 35, 50, 52, 64, 65, 70,
    93, 155
Stalin, Josef, 26, 174
Stepney, Rob, 29, 78, 79, 98, 100,
    103, 119, 120, 121, 122, 123,
    138
Stylites, Simeon, 94, 96, 97
Suetonius, 60
Suicide, 102, 104
Surgeon General of the United
    States, 134

T

Tacitus, 60
Tame, Dr Chris R., 2, v, xv, xix,
    xx
Tezcatlipoca, 49, 52
Thatcher, Margaret Hilda, xiv, 29,
    78, 119, 127, 129
Theodosius, Emperor, xviii, 80,
    95
Times, The, 24, 31, 45, 78, 79,
    102, 119, 123, 124, 125, 128,
    132, 134, 136, 137, 170
Tobacco Chamber, 59
Toleration, 81, 108
Tollison, Robert D., 165, 167
Tonoupinambaultiis tribe, 49
Toynbee, Polly, 102
Trimalchio, 32

U

United Kingdom, 23, 120, 125
United States, 69, 72, 73, 134,